TRAIL OF A YANKEE

From the diaries of Samuel Jones Melvin,
a young private in the Union Army during the Civil War

with additional notes and
commentary from his grandson
Paul C. Melvin

Copyright 2025 by Richard Melvin

All rights reserved. This book or any portion thereof may not be reproduced or used in any manner whatsoever without the express written permission of the publisher except for the use of brief quotations in a book review.

Richard Melvin, LLC
Hilliard, OH 43026

ISBN: 978-1-7349030-6-5

DEDICATION

Samuel Jones Melvin, circa 1900

This book is about Samuel Jones Melvin, who served as an enlisted man in the Union Army during the Civil War. The content in this book comes from Samuel's diaries, with additional commentary from my father Paul C. Melvin. Dad's commentary ties things together and brings the story to life. That commentary comes from a 99-page typewritten manuscript that Dad wrote in the 1960s, using his beloved Underwood typewriter.

I, along with my sister Pam and brothers Brad and Randy, shall forever be grateful that Dad wrote this manuscript. It preserves an important part of our family's legacy and forms the foundation for this book.

Richard Paul Melvin
Samuel's Great-Grandson

Paul C. Melvin, Samuel's Grandson

The Title Page of Dad's Manuscript

Table of Contents

About This Book 5

Meet the Author 9

1862: Drafted into the Union Army 11

The Roundheads 24

1863: Fighting the Rebs and His Health 27

1864: More Health Problems, Then Back to the War 49

1865: Heavy Fighting, and Finally Back Home 85

1866: Back Home, and a Romance Begins 127

Epilogue 129

About This Book

by Richard Melvin

Samuel Jones Melvin was my great-grandfather. He kept a daily diary starting on January 1, 1861, when he was only twenty-two years old. He wrote in his diary every day for fifty-one years until his final entry, which he wrote on June 2, 1913, just before he passed away.

As I got into my 70s, I realized that our family had a tremendous legacy resource in the form of these diaries. They were contained in an old wooden bookcase, perfectly sized to hold them. Samuel had carefully labeled and stored these little books in this bookcase, and my father and grandfather had lovingly protected them as the years passed. Each book has a small label on it to mark the year.

I set up a photo studio in a spare bedroom and began the task of digitally preserving these old diaries for our family. I used a Canon EOS 70D DSLR camera for this work, saving the files on a dedicated hard drive and backing them up off-site. I shot a total of 6,316 images of diary pages in my little photo studio. Professional archivists might scoff at this amateur setup, but it worked fine. The diaries are now preserved in high-resolution, easy-to-read digital files for our family's future generations.

The production of this book became a multi-generational, collaborative family project. The family members' contributions were:

- Samuel Jones Melvin's original diary entries

- Grandson Paul Melvin's 99-page, typed manuscript with additional commentary

- Great-grandson Richard's design work in laying out this book

- Great-granddaughter Pamela Gast's copyediting and proofreading to make sure this book complies with *The Chicago Manual of Style*

- Great-grandsons Brad and Randy Melvin and great-great-granddaughter Carrie Drovdlic's work with the layout proofs during production to check for layout errors, typos, misplaced captions, and so forth

This book is the result of those collaborative efforts.

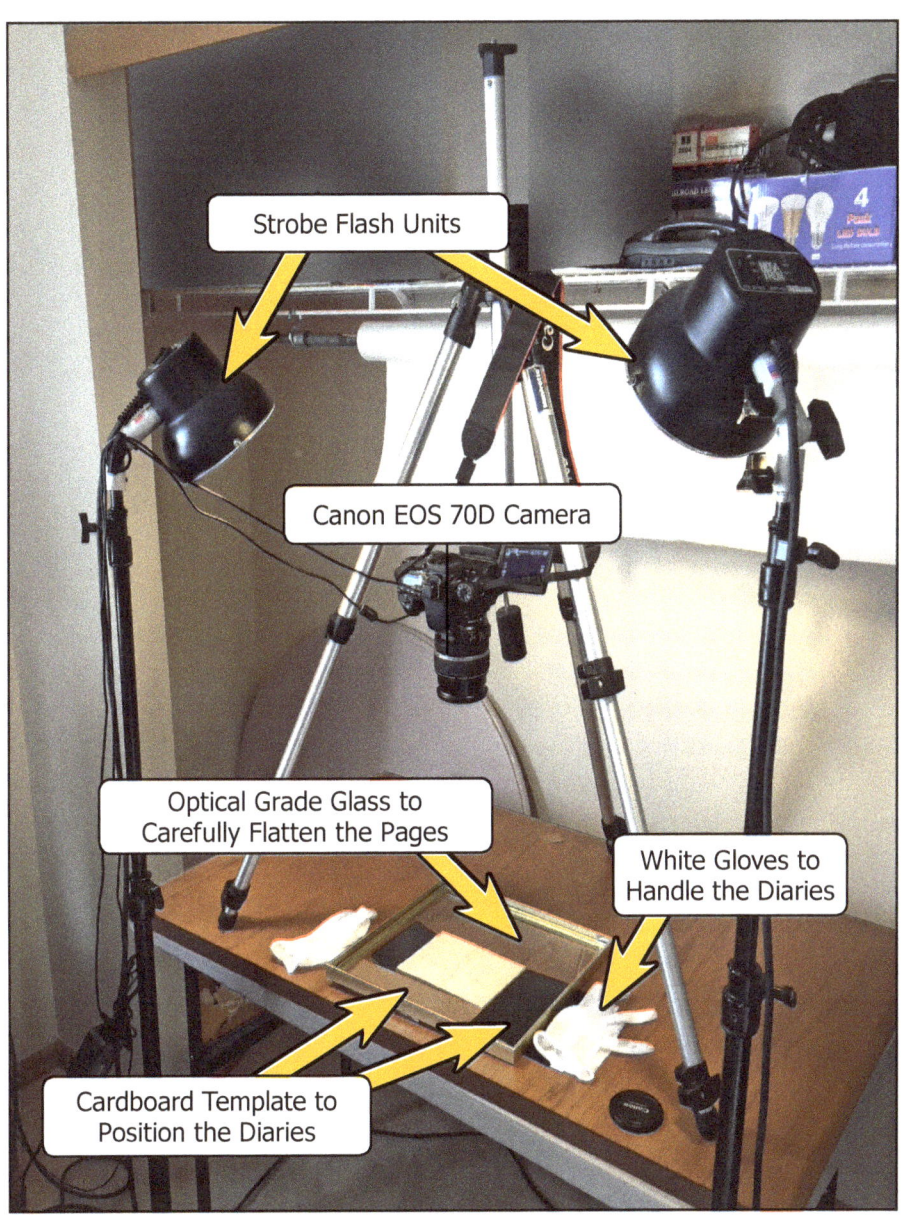

The Diary Preservation Photo Studio

Our Multi-Generational, Collaborative Family in 2025

Meet the Author

by Paul C. Melvin

Allow me to introduce my grandfather, Samuel Jones Melvin. I never met my Grandfather Melvin. He died before I was born. However, I feel that I know him well. You see, when he died he left fifty-two diaries, daily accounts of his life from his college days in 1861 until he died fifty-two years later. He was a Union soldier in the Civil War, and that is the period of his life this book is all about. Through his own writing, you will discover how life was in Civil wartime, and what it was like to be soldier in Company A, Roundhead Regiment, 100th Pennsylvania Volunteers.

This is a true story about the experiences of a young private in the Union Army during the Civil War. The daily entries in his diaries tell of what was happening to him and to those around him. He relates his feelings as he moves in and out of battle—truly a day-by-day account of his story.

Grandfather was a student at Adrian College in Michigan when the Civil War began. He was needed on the farm back home near Eldersville, Pennsylvania. He left college and went home to help his father farm the hilly, rough ground when it happened on October 18, 1862.

But I'll let him tell you in his own words.

Samuel Jones Melvin and Family, circa 1910
Front Row: Helen and Samuel Melvin
Back Row: Charles, Mary, Alice, and Galbraith (my Father)

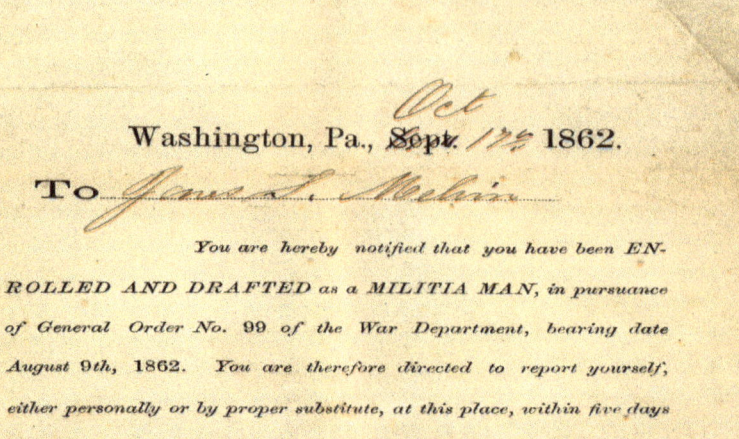

Samuel's draft notice

Note that his draft notice was addressed to
"Jones S. Melvin" instead of "Samuel J. Melvin."

Also, the date was scratched out and changed from September to October.
Based upon Samuel's diary entry, the correct date was October 18, 1862.

1862: Drafted into the Union Army

Saturday, October 18, 1862
Heard about noon that I was drafted. Took no offense at it whatever but concluded to go cheerfully trusting in God. Went to town in the evening. Drafted men taking it very hard, some wanting substitutes. Very fine day.

You see, in those days it was possible for a man who was drafted in the army to pay another man to go to war in his place. It was legal, but not wholly acceptable. Grandfather chose to serve himself. He could not think of allowing someone else to put himself in harm's way for him. So he enlisted, and a few days later writes:

Wednesday, October 22, 1862
Delivered up the account of my school and father & I went to Washington. Was there sworn into Co. A Round Head Regiment.

He went off to war six days later when he wrote:

Tuesday, October 28, 1862
Father read the XXXIV Psalm at family worship, and I soon bade farewell with those remaining at home and went with father, Mary & Lyd [his sister and cousin] *to Steubenville* [Ohio] *on my way to war. Got to Pittsburg* [sic] *about four o'clock. Went to the Provost Marshal and was sent to the Newroth House and spent the night very comfortably on U.S. fair* [sic] [food]. *The bar had bottles on the shelf and men came in and drank when they felt like it. . . . Felt rather peculiar.*

Wednesday, October 29, 1862
Spent forenoon in the Provost Marshal's office. [His enlistment papers were being processed.] *At 8-20 P.M. we started for Harrisburgh* [sic]. *Accident happened. Locomotive ran off the track and was ruined. No one hurt. Campaigners* [soldiers] *in cars swearing and drunken. Saw an affecting scene of a drunken Irishman parting with his wife and children. He had been in the guardhouse all day. Thought seriously of my future destiny.*

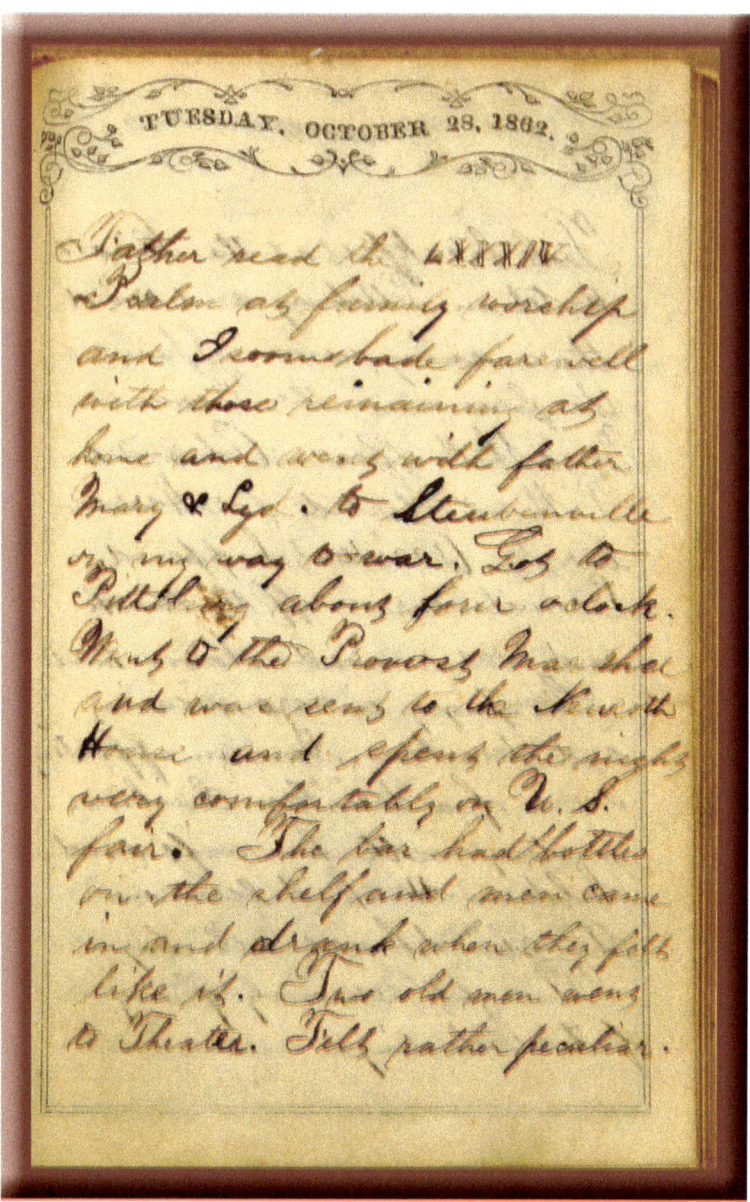

October 28, 1862: Off to serve in the the Union Army

Well, so much for his first day in the army. Now he begins to settle into the army routine. It's a new way of life for a small-town farm boy who had never been away from home any length of time except to attend college in Adrian, Michigan. But he was a man who accepted life as it happened and tried to make the best of it. We pick up his comments twenty-four hours later:

Thursday, October 30, 1862
Camp Curtin. Took a soldier's dinner at Camp Curtin [Harrisburg]. Was rather hard to take. Crackers, beef & soup. . . . Slept in camp for the first time. Slept comfortably.

Friday, October 31, 1862
Camp Curtin: Washed myself at the hydren [sic] in the morning, attended at roll call, ate breakfast, which tasted good although different from what I was used to. . . . Slept very comfortably on a hard bunk in barracks B. O that the men would cease to take the name of the Lord in vain.

Grandfather was a very religious man. His home life ill prepared him for some of the people he would meet during his army days. He was used to early to bed, early to rise, work hard all day, take regular, well-cooked meals, go to church on Sundays (twice, sometimes three times) and midweek prayer meetings.

Saturday, November 1, 1862
Camp Curtin. Attended roll call in the morning and was called on guard by the sergeant and the Capt. ordered me out until I should receive uniform. Was not able to procure a uniform during the day.

He had misplaced his enlistment papers. No papers, no uniform. He could not prove to the Captain that he belonged there. So he wanders around the area and comments on what he sees.

Saw a man play the fife and his two boys, one five, the other eight years old, play the drums. A haughty captain ordered them out, but the adjutant told them to play on. Card playing carried on in the barracks at night, and great profanity.

Tuesday, November 4, 1862
Camp Curtin. After breakfast and roll call in the morning, I was sent to be sent with a squad to town for my papers, but was entirely neglected. Passed the time away until afternoon and spent an hour or so at head quarters. Found my papers, drew my clothing and went out on dress parade. . . . Discovered lice in the barracks.

Now he was settling in. He felt more a member of the outfit. His captain accepted him. He had his training assignment and had begun to form friendships, some of which would last a lifetime. The men were becoming a fighting unit. They were learning to depend on each other, trusting each other, looking out for each other—which leads to this entry:

Friday, November 7, 1862
Camp Curtin. Arose at the usual hour and as Sergeant Humel started taking my blanket I recaptured it. Was appointed Assistant sergeant of barracks B. . . . Two cooks got drunk and we had a big time putting them to bed to keep them out of the guard house. . . . Felt comfortable in my bunk at night.

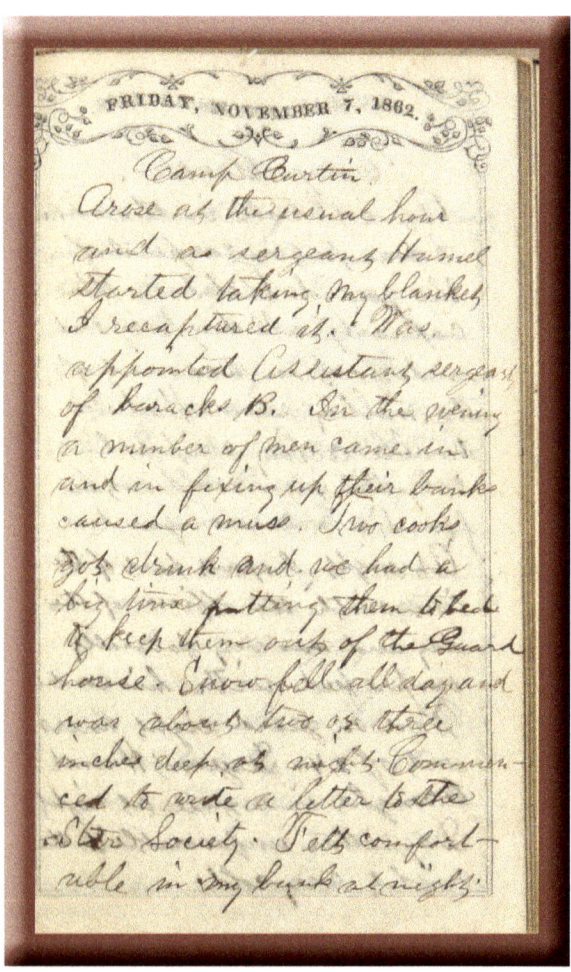

November 7, 1862: The cooks get drunk.

The Melvin Family Home circa 1860

So begins the tedious routine of army life. Orders come for transfer, and he writes:

Tuesday, November 11, 1862
Baltimore. At dress parade in the morning my name among others was called, and we were soon before headquarters receiving our rations to start to our regiments. . . . Started at half past one. Soldiers all in hind car. Little better crowd than came from Pittsburg [sic] to harrisburg [sic]. Got to Baltimore about seven o'clock.

Wednesday, November 12, 1862
Washington, DC Left Baltimore about ten o'clock after taking a very good substantial breakfast at the Union Relief association. Breakfast of beef, bread, cabbage and coffee.

He was off to Washington D.C., a very tedious trip because their cars were coupled to the end of a slow-moving, frequently stopping freight train. A day later he writes:

Thursday, November 13, 1862
Camp Recruit, Alexandria. Found no wood in camp. Had to gather brush for bed and wood. Got us a good supper after so long a time.

Then, on November 15, comes this startling entry:

Saturday, November 15, 1862
Camp Recruit, Alexandria. Man stabbed at night and killed.

Sunday, November 16, 1862
Camp Recruit. Arose early and got breakfast. . . . we took our Bibles in the form of a bible class and made remarks. Felt much encouraged and favorably impressed with our squad. Knapsack inspection in the forenoon. Saw the man who committed murder, led out of camp to be tried. . . . Some of the boys had the mumps.

Monday, November 17, 1862
Camp Recruit. Nothing very interesting occurred in the afternoon, but about bedtime Montgomery missed his pocket book. Search was immediately instituted and Keefer suspected. After we were all examined, we took him to the [captain's] *tent where endeavored to bring me into the scrape, but failed; He went and brought the money, was ironed and put in the guard house, and we went to bed.*

And so it went—training, eating, sleeping, trying to keep as comfortable as possible in the cold autumn air. Winter is fast approaching and his unit is moved south. The next meaningful entry:

Monday, December 1, 1862
Camp near Fredericksburg. Drilled some in the manual of arms. Procured my gun the one Ben Stewart used to carry.

Up to this time, guns (muskets) were not available for training, only for men getting close to combat. This entry is a puzzle. Evidently this musket was issued to a Ben Stewart before it was reissued to grandfather. Speculation is that Mr. Stewart was killed and his musket given to grandfather.

Samuel's Springfield Model 1816 Musket

Samuel's Gun

Samuel's great-grandson Randall Melvin is the caretaker of Samuel's gun. Randy's research shows that this gun is a Springfield Model 1816, 69-caliber, smooth-bore musket. It was manufactured in 1828 as a flintlock, then was later converted to percussion action. This gun was already obsolete during the Civil War.

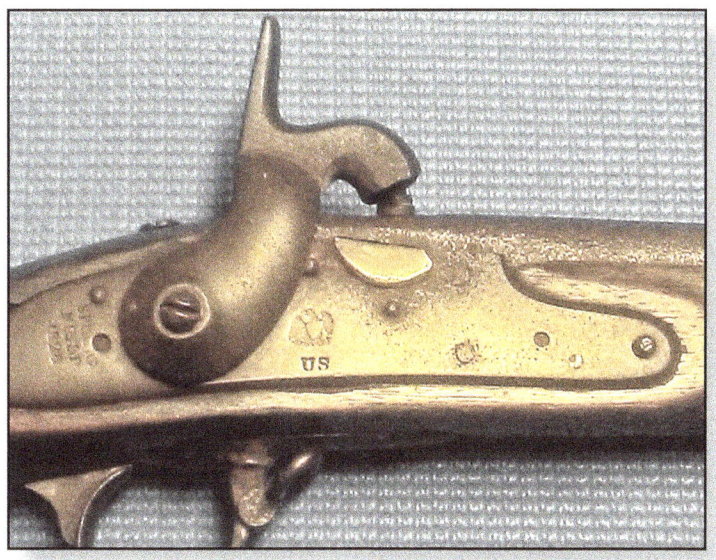

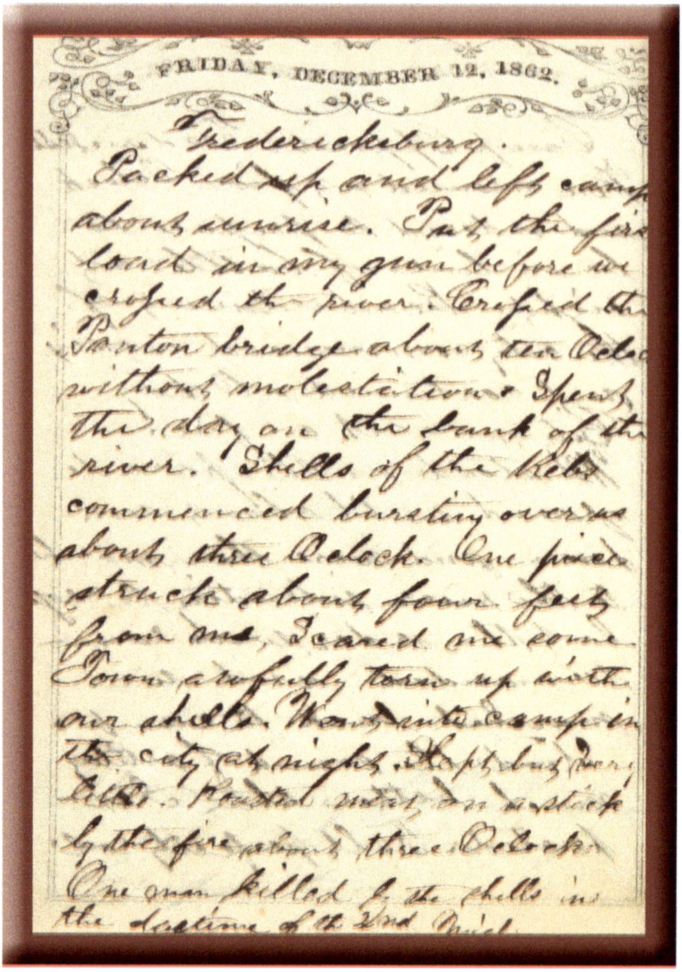

December 12, 1862: Under fire for the first time

The line of battle in Fredericksburg (Library of Congress)

The days of preparation for battle go on. The entries are the same—wake, eat, drill, sleep—day after day. Then comes the call to battle:

Thursday, December 11, 1862

Camp Opposite Fredericksburg. Were aroused at five o'clock and ordered to prepare to be in line of battle at eight. Bombardment of the city [Fredericksburg] *commenced at six and continued all day. City was set on fire. We stood on the parade ground until about sundown and were then marched to the river intending to cross, but the order was countermanded and we marched back to camp. Stood the sound of artillery much better than I expected. Felt perfectly cool.*

This was his first introduction to battle. He was in a reserve unit ready to be reinforcements to the front-line fighting, but the order into battle never came—this time. But the next day:

Friday, December 12, 1862

Fredericksburg. Packed up and left camp about sunrise. Put the first load in my gun before we crossed the river. Crossed Pouton bridge about ten o'clock without molestation. [no one wounded or killed]. *Spent the day on the bank of the river. Shells of the Rebs commenced bursting over us about three o'clock. One piece struck about four feet from me. Scared me some.* [These were what might be considered anti-personnel shells, which were loaded with metal fragments and set to explode over the soldier's heads and rain down upon them to either kill or maim.] *Town awfully torn up with our shells. Went into camp in the city at night. Slept but very little. . . . One man killed by the shells in the daytime.*

Saturday, December 13, 1862

Fredericksburg. Took arms about half past eight o'clock and marched about two miles. Were placed to support a battery. . . . The fight raged terrifically all around us. We did not fire a gun. . . . Reb's left flank was turned. Saw some prisoners taken across the bridge. Firing continued after dark.

Fredericksburg Pickets (Library of Congress)

Sunday, December 14, 1862
Fredericksburg. Marched from our position in the morning along the river bank of the Rapahannock [sic] *and halted until near noon when we formed in a line of battle at the bridge in front of the town.* [Fredericksburg] *Here we spent the afternoon waiting for orders. Chaplain of our regiment held services in the afternoon.* [His unit fully expected to be thrown into the front line battle for Fredericksburg.] *About sunset we were marched back near where we were in the morning and spent the night there. Felt ready to go into battle, but was glad we were not called on. Very heavy fighting during the day.*

Tuesday, December 16, 1862
Camp Opposite Fredericksburg. Drew the ball out of my gun and washed the barrel out. Some of the James Island prisoners came to us. Slept very comfortably after attending prayers.

    The action had quieted down some in his sector; and things seemed to settle into routine operations of readiness, inspections, prayer meetings, and receiving prisoners being brought back from the front. But some action came on December 22:

Monday, December 22, 1862
Camp Opposite Fredericksburg. Went on reserve picket duty at nine o'clock. Had a comfortable place. . . . Gathered some grass and pine brush for a bed. . . . Did not sleep much on account of pain in my back and bowells [sic]. *Rained a few drops near daylight. Some doubts about what such strong picketing* [observing] *was for.*

> **What is Picket Duty?**
> Picket duty was similar to guard duty. Your post was forward of your lines and usually in a good hiding place or in a shallow hole in the ground covered with brush—a forward lookout post to observe enemy front line activity.

Now it's Christmas Eve, a time when he longs to be home with family and friends, but the soldiers had to make the best of things. Here's what he wrote:

Wednesday, December 24, 1862
Camp Near Fredericksburg. Some of the boys were making preparations for Christmas by buying whiskey. Some very drunk. Attended prayer service and read a tract. [A tract is a small pamphlet of religious origin.]

Christmas morning came—his first away from home. He's a young man used to celebrating Christmas with a Christmas tree, decorated home, festive music, church services, delicious food, and comfortable surroundings. But not this Christmas!

Thursday, December 25, 1862
Camp Opposite Fredericksburg. [in pup tents, two men to a tent sleeping on the ground—cold and windy] *Was very unwell during the forenoon. Ate five scorched crackers and drank some coffee for breakfast. Spent most of the forenoon in the tent. . . . Did not eat any dinner. Took supper of fat pork, onions, crackers, and coffee.* [Not very good Christmas fare, but it was considered good field rations in those days.] *Attended prayers in the evening, and the chaplain made some very appropriate remarks in reference to the birth of Christ, and the manner in which Christmas is generally spent. Firing was heard on the opposite side of the river in the evening late which we did not understand.*

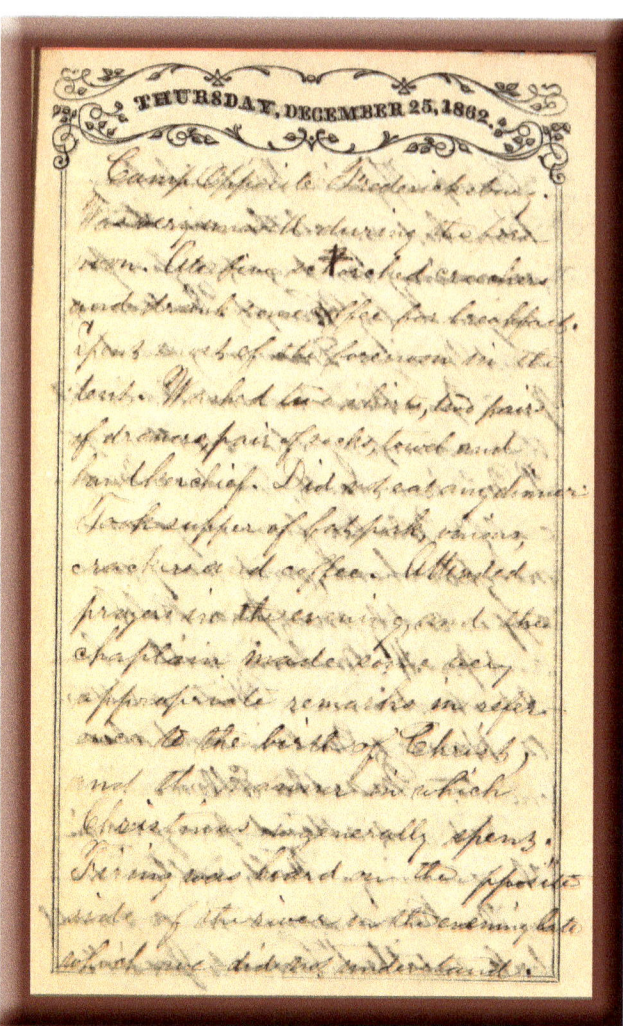

Christmas 1862 in a pup tent

His entries comment on his feeling of unwellness. He is cold. His body aches. It's wet, and his entry on December 30 says:

Tuesday, December 30, 1862
Camp Opposite Fredericksburg. Spent most of the afternoon in the tent. Bought some soft bread. . . . Wrote a letter to father and mother in the evening. Had a very troublesome cough which made me feel bad. Rained in the evening.

A small group of wounded Union soldiers rest outside a hospital in Fredericksburg, Virginia. The woman seated in doorway is volunteer nurse Abby Hopper Gibbons from New York City. Samuel may have known some of these men.
(Library of Congress)

Wednesday, December 31, 1862

Camp Opposite Fredericksburg. Felt rather unwell in the morning, but packed my blankets in a knapsack and went on picket with a number of the boys of Co. A. . . . Rebs kept perfectly quiet. Was on post with Sam Thompson and A.C. McKeever. My first time on post. . . . A.C and I talked some of the pleasures of home. This ends my experience in the year of our Lord 1862.

The grinding boredom and tedium of an army standing and waiting for something to happen sets in. He is cold, wet, and hungry because the food is not all that good.

So ends the year of 1862.

The Roundheads

(Library of Congress)

Samuel served in the One Hundredth Pennsylvania Volunteers regiment. They were more commonly known as the Roundhead Regiment. This regiment recruited men from the southwestern counties of Pennsylvania.
The Roundheads became a reality in August of 1861 when Daniel Leasure, a native of New Castle, Pennsylvania, received authority to recruit a regiment of infantry.

Ultimately twelve companies were recruited for this regiment. They initially formed up at Camp Wilkins in Pittsburgh. Field officers were soon commissioned. They included Colonel Daniel Leasure, Lieutenant Colonel James Armstrong, and Major David A. Leckey. As the ranking officer, Colonel Leasure was placed in command of the brigade.

Throughout 1863 and 1864 the regiment served the Union Army well and was directly involved in several significant battles.

On the morning of March 25, 1865, the rebels attacked Fort Steadman. The Roundheads were engaged in this battle, and Lieutenant Colonel Joseph H. Pentecost was killed. (See Samuel's diary entries for March 25-27, 1865, on page 53.) The 100th's final battle of the war was in Petersburg, Virginia, on April 2, 1865. It was a decisive battle in favor of the Union army, and a bad day for the rebels.

Soon after this battle, the regiment returned to City Point. They then went to Washington and on to Harrisburg where the regiment was mustered out of service on July 21, 1865.

The Roundheads Civil War Engagements

100TH REGIMENT

Organized Aug. 31, 1861.   Re-Enlisted Jan. 1, 1864
Mustered Out July 24, 1865

ENGAGEMENTS

Port Royal, S. C.	Nov. 7, 1861
Port Royal Ferry, S. C.	Jan. 1, 1862
James Island, S. C.	June 3 and 16, 1862
Bull Run, Va.	Aug. 29 and 30, 1862
Chantilly, Va.	Sept. 1, 1862
South Mountain, Md.	Sept. 14, 1862
Antietam, Md.	Sept. 17, 1862
Fredericksburg, Va.	Dec. 12 and 13, 1862
Siege of Vicksburg, Miss.	June 15 to July 4, '63
Jackson, Miss.	July 11 to 15, 1863
Blue Springs, Tenn.	Oct. 10, 1863
Campbell Station, Tenn.	Nov. 16, 1863
Siege of Knoxville, Tenn.	Nov. 18 to Dec 5, '63
Fort Sanders, Tenn.	Nov. 29, 1863
Wilderness, Va.	May 6, 1864
Spottsylvania, Va.	May 12, 1864
North Ann River, Va.	May 23, 1864
Bethesda Church Va.	June 1, 1864
Cold Harber, Va.	June 2, 1864
Petersburg, Va.	June 17, 1864
Mine Explosion, Va.	July 30, 1864
Weldon Rail Road, Va.	Aug. 19 and 21, '64
Poplar Grove Church, Va.	Sept. 30, 1864
Hatcher's Run, Va.	Oct. 27, 1864
Fort Stedman, Va.	March 25, 1865
Final Assault on Petersburg, Va.	April 2,' 65

Wounded Union soldiers relaxing near the hospital in Fredericksburg, Virginia
(Library of Congress)

1863: Fighting the Rebs and His Health

The first of the year has come and gone. 1863 is over a week old. He has been on almost continuous picket duty since New Year's Eve.

Friday, January 9, 1863
Camp Opposite Fredericksburg. Went on picket at 9 o'clock. Only on post from 10 until 12 P.M.. Two men drowned crossing the river contrary to orders, after exchanging newspapers with the Rebs. One body was recovered. Rebs sent note over by sail asking to exchange tobacco for coffee.

It was common practice to call across the lines of battle during lulls in the fighting. Many times tobacco, whiskey, and newspapers were exchanged back and forth. Sometimes soldiers from both sides would gather between the lines to talk and sing to the accompaniment of a guitar, mouthharp, mouth organ, or banjo. Then they would return to their lines to await orders to begin fighting again.

The Bombardment of Fredericksburg (Library of Congress)

His various ailments were affecting his ability as a fighting man. His entry for January 25 reads:

Sunday, January 25, 1863
Camp Opposite Fredericksburg. On picket in morning. Rained about four o'clock. Was not able to keep up with the company coming in. Feet and knees very painful. . . . Did not attend prayers on account of my pains.

Monday, January 26, 1863
Camp Opposite Fredericksburg. Reported at hospital. . . . Could scarcely get about. . . . Gathered some grass for bed. News of Bursides [sic] *removal. Hooker in command. . . Felt unwell in evening.*

At this point he is exempted from duty. He celebrates his 24th birthday on February 6, 1863, in the hospital, still excused from duty. It's very cold and snowing.

February brings about some changes:

Saturday, February 7, 1863
Camp Opposite Fredericksburg. Was put on light duty by the Doctor in the morning. Carried a small load of wood. Carried some water and washed my clothes.

Tuesday, February 10, 1863
On Board the Sylvan Shore. Broke up camp opposite Fredericksburg about noon. Got on board the cars [a passenger train] *at five o'clock (on a hog car) and landed at Aquia Creek Where we boarded the boat. . . . Could not keep up with the company on march.*

Thursday, February 12, 1863
On Board the Sylvan Shore. Considerable water in the boat. Heavy wind in the night..

Friday, February 13, 1863
New Port News [Virginia]. *Landed off the Sylvan Shore about eleven o'clock. . . . Marched about 1 ½ miles and pitched our tents. Had to follow the regiment. Rheumatism so bad. Cut some grass for a bed.*

At this point he is feeling badly with the rheumatism. His whole body aches. His joints and legs are very painful. It's cold. It's damp.

Sunday, February 15, 1863
New Port News. Felt miserable with rheumatism. Day very cool. No fire in our tent.

Here he is reporting to the hospital daily due to his mounting aches and pains. He's only twenty four years old, but the rugged life of living in a wet, cold tent and sleeping on the ground has taken its toll. He is in and out of the hospital. He was either excused from duty or on light duty. He is assigned to the hospital and still a private on the line. He is working in the wards helping with the wounded.

Wednesday, April 8, 1863
Hospital No. 1. Ward No 7 Lexington Ky. Regiment ordered to pack up at 7 o'clock. Reported to Doctor. Gathered up my things and put them in the ambulance, and when we got to hospital by request I got to work. Put in charge of Ward No. 7. . . . Felt it a responsible position to deal out medicine and care for the rooms . . . Did not sleep much.

Sunday, April 12, 1863
Hospital No 1 Ward No. 7 Lexington Ky. Arose at 5 o'clock, made beds, changed bed clothes in room, cleaned up for inspection with no one to help me. Administered medicine as usual and did not sit down until two o'clock. Wanted to go to church but could not. Felt very tired and weak.

Monday, April 13, 1863
Hospital No. 1 Lexington Kentucky. Felt very weak and unable to attend to the sick as they should be attended to but did my best. Asked for help but it was refused further than what I could raise in my own ward. Felt that I was imposed upon.

Thursday, April 16, 1863
General Hospital No. 1 Lexington Ky. Got a good dinner from a darky woman near hospital for 25 ct. . . . Old man Clark died in our ward.

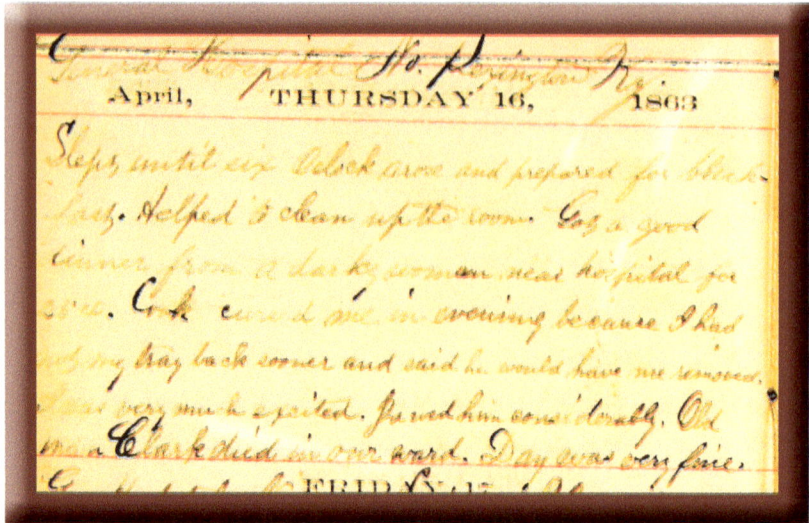
April 16, 1863: A good dinner and a death in the ward

Sunday, April 19, 1863
General Hospital No. 1 Lexington Ky. Attended Catholic church in the forenoon and got very tired of the ceremony. . . . Attended the colored church and heard sermon from darkie from Rev. III 20th. Exciting time.

Monday, April 20, 1863
Hospital No 1 Lexington Kentucky. Bought my breakfast from a darkie woman. Spent the forenoon about the yard of the hospital, felt lonely. . . . No letters from home. Don't know why.

Thursday, April 23, 1863
Convalescent Camp Lexington Kentucky. Was put on guard in the evening. Guarding a prisoner who was arrested for writing a letter to the President concerning his discharge.

Tuesday, April 28, 1863
Convalescent Camp, Lexington Kentucky. Volunteered for work in the morning. Was sent to town with a wagon for lumber. Went twice and could not get it. Saw a lady who had disguised herself and acted soldier several months and was afterward arrested as a spy, but was cleared.

The days drag on. He indicates that the camp has quieted down some because all the "rowdies" are put in jail.

Tuesday, May 5, 1863
Convalescent Camp Lexington Kentucky. Medical Director inspected us in the afternoon and marked me for my regiment.

Sunday, May 10, 1863
Convalescent Camp Lexington Kentucky. Went on smallpox guard at two o'clock and came off at four.

   This entry is not clear as to what *smallpox guard* was. There may have been a smallpox outbreak nearby and guards were set out to keep any infected people from entering the camp. Smallpox killed many soldiers in the Civil War, so the precautions were probably very necessary.

   Now they were on the move—fast—getting up early to march. They marched until noon, ate, and marched some more until late afternoon, then stopped for the night. They were moving fast to some place—they knew not where. The entries are short with little information except to note the day and the fact that they were marching. He notes that it was rainy, cold, windy, and he is keeping up with the rest of the regiment quite well.

Wednesday, May 27, 1863
Camp near Columbia Ky. Got marching orders about three o'clock, and all our regiment, the 36th Mass. and two pieces of artillery started and marched until half past one o'clock. Slept in a meadow on the Glascow road.

Friday, May 29, 1863
Scouting in Kentucky. At half past nine o'clock we started on the march, and halted at Breading [sic] *at two. . . . We were very wet and cold. . . . Some firing heard, but we did not hear what for.*

Saturday, May 30, 1863
Camp Near Columbia. Were drawn up to meet the rebels but they were not there. Marched to camp after night. Got in about one o'clock. . . . Eight rebels captured and six horses, very nice ones.

   Grandfather, coming from the farm, was assigned to taking care of the mules that pulled the wagons. The men who cared for the mules were known as "mule skinners."

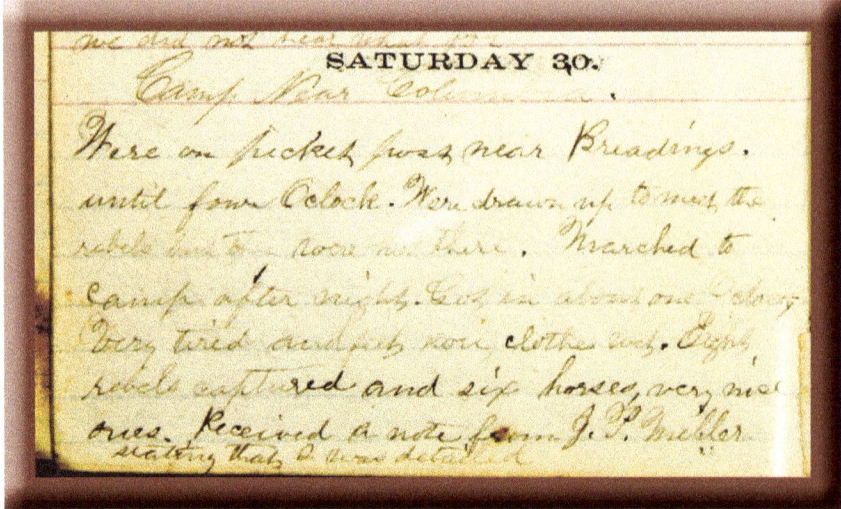

May 30, 1863: Captured eight rebels and six horses

Monday, June 1, 1863
Corelle between Columbia and Lebanon. Arose at two o'clock took breakfast, helped to hitch up some mules, spent the day with the wagon train between Columbia and Lebanon. Dove [sic] six mules most of the way. Spent the night with James Thompson in his wagon.

A captain discovered Grandfather writing in his diary and was very surprised to find a man who could read and write, and was also college educated. The captain ordered him to report to headquarters.

Samuel's Handwriting

When the Captain observed Samuel writing in his diary, he was very impressed. However, it seems that Samuel had a somewhat plain writing style for his diary entries, and another style for more formal writing.

His formal writing style was a work of art. For example, here is his signature as he wrote it on a book of writing he did while studying at Adrian College.

He was assigned to the Headquarters Company as a clerk because he could read and write . . . and what is he doing? He's driving a headquarters wagon with a six-mule team. He is ordered to Louisville, evidently alone.

Tuesday, June 2, 1863
Louisville Kentucky. Got on the cars at half past one o'clock and landed in Louisville at 7. . . . Could not get out to see the city on account of the guards.

Wednesday, June 3, 1863
Louisville, Kentucky. Was kept in the barracks all day. . . . Felt lonesome and wanted to be going. . . . Chaplain H.H. White held service in the barracks in the evening.

He gives no reason for the confinement to barracks. There could have been a quarantine of some kind. However, the next day the outfit is ordered to the railway station.

Thursday, June 4, 1863
Hd. Qrs. Lexington Kentucky. Arose at four o'clock and took breakfast, got on board the cars [train] *at Louisville at 7 oc. passed through some very fine country through Frankfort about eleven Oc, arrived in Lex at one. Went to Convalescent Camp and got my descriptive list.*

A *descriptive list* from this era was the equivalent of a modern medical record. It contained all the information about Grandfather's prior medical issues while he was in Virginia.

Friday, June 5, 1863
Hd Qrs. 9th A.C. Lexington Kentucky. Did some writing in the A.A. Gen's Office. Received my descriptive list from Captain Pentecost. . . . Had some serious apprehensions of going to Vicksburg. Felt lonesome.

During the spring and summer of 1863, the siege of Vicksburg, Mississippi, took place. The prize here was establishing full control of the Mississippi River. Control of the river was vital to military operations west of the Appalachian mountain range. The Union Army had control of almost all of the river, except for about two miles of the waterway at Vicksburg. Consequently, fighting here was vicious as the Confederates vigorously defended their stronghold on the river and the bluffs east of the city. Samuel knew this, which is why he expressed his concerns for going there.

Union troops attempted to dig a canal across the peninsula opposite Vicksburg to allow boats to bypass the Confederate batteries. But the canal project ultimately failed, and this plan was abandoned.

Union troops digging a canal to bypass Vicksburg.
It was never completed. (Library of Congress)

One of General Sherman's batteries in Vicksburg (Library of Congress)

The Battle of Vicksburg is considered a turning point in the Civil War. President Lincoln said, *"Vicksburg is the key. The war can never be brought to a close until that key is in our pocket."* The fighting at Vicksburg went on for over a year, but when that battle was finally won by the Union Army, the outcome of the Civil War was no longer in doubt.

President Abraham Lincoln
(Library of Congress)

Evidently about this time Samuel is beginning to settle in at Headquarters Company, and he is being given more clerk-type work to do. From here on for a while the action at Headquarters is hectic. The Confederate Army is everywhere it seems. And some elements of that army are trying to capture the Union Army Field Headquarters. They are constantly packing, unpacking, or moving—but I'll let him tell you about it.

A confederate gun defending Vicksburg (Library of Congress)

Wednesday, June 10, 1863
On Board Packet Express. Went on shore at Cannelton, Ind. On Indiana soil for the first time. . . . Rather lonely in the tent.

Thursday, June 11, 1863
On Board Packet Express. Landed at Cairo, Ill about half past five o'clock. . . . Much disappointed in the appearance of the place. Bought some onions and sausage.

He stayed on the boat for several days. The entries are not very exciting. He tends to keep mostly to the bow watching the Mississippi roll by. They land at Memphis to take on coal, lay over for the night, and then move on toward Milldale, Mississippi.

Saturday, June 20, 1863
Hd. Qrs. 9th A.C. Milldale Mississippi. Saw a great light in the direction of Vicksburg after dark. Thought the town on fire. Still no word of the Assistant Quarter Master.

This is another puzzling entry. He did not note anywhere that the Assistant Quarter Master was missing. Now, out of nowhere, comes a surprise entry:

General Ulysses S. Grant
(Library of Congress)

Sunday, June 21, 1863
Hd. Qrs. Co. 9th A.C. Milldale Miss. . . . Saw Genl' [sic] *U.S. Grant in the afternoon.*

Monday, June 22, 1863
Hd. Qrs. Co. 9th A.C. Milldale Mississippi. Our desks still being behind, I had nothing particular to do. Visited Company A and learned that Gen'l Lee was invading Pennsylvania, and was only nine miles from Harrisburg. . . . Our forces digging entrenchments on the hills near Methodist Church in which Chief Q.M.'s office was. Ordered to be ready to move.

Tuesday, June 23, 1863
Hd. Qrs. Co. 9th A.C. Milldale Mississippi. Moved Head Qarters [sic] *in the forenoon back from the church toward the Yazoo River.*

Thursday, June 25, 1863
Hd. Qrs. Co. 9th A.C. Milldale Mississippi. Copied a number of orders. Went out on the hill in the evening and listened to the fighting at Vicksburg. Musketry [gun fire] *could be heard distinctly. Took a wash. Could not sleep much on account of mosquitoes.*

On June 26, 1863, Union troops blew up one of the rebel forts in Vicksburg and made a charge through the breach. The pressed the rebels on every side, and they realized that further resistance was hopeless. They surrendered Vicksburg on July 4, 1863, after a siege of 65 days. (Library of Congress)

Several entries during this time contain the phrase "could not sleep." Evidently his duties at Headquarters, the change in his assignment, the men fighting and dying nearby all weighed heavily on his mind, but:

Monday, June 29, 1863
Hd. Qrs. 9th A.C. Reaf [plunder] *of Vicksburg A.O.R.* [Army of the Republic] *Were aroused at four o'clock in the morning. Issued marching orders to each of the divisions. . . . Marching was hard. Roads awful dusty. Very many of the troops fell out by the way. Stopped at two or three different houses and found the inhabitants there.*

Saturday, July 4, 1863
Hd Qrs 9th A.C. Near Oak Ridge Miss. Heard by telegraph that Vicksburg had surrendered. Visited the regiments in the evening. Found them preparing to move.

Vicksburg Surrenders on July 4, 1863 (Library of Congress)

Sunday, July 5, 1863
Hd Qrs Co. 9th A.C . Bear Creek Mississippi. Packed up our things in the morning and moved from camp at 9 A.M. Very warm & roads dusty. . . . Halted about sundown and pitched our tent on Bear Creek. . . . Cannons firing was heard about ten o'clock P.M. Our troops putting a bridge across Big black river.

The city of Vicksburg, circa 1863 (Library of Congress)

Riverboats docked in Vicksburg, circa 1863 (Library of Congress)

Monday, July 6, 1863
Hd. Qrs. 9th A.C. Near Big Black River Mississippi. Prepared to move Head Quarters. Went to fill the canteens and lost my coat containing my diary, bible, and a number of letters. Felt very badly about it. Thunderstorm in the evening. Pitched our tent about dark and did not have much to do.

Tuesday, July 7, 1863
Hd. Quarters' Way on train Near Meisenger's [sic] *Ferry* [Messenger's Ferry] *Were routed in the morning at 3-20 by an orderly from Gen. Sherman stating that the enemy were still scattered and we must strike immediately. The bridge at Birdsong's not being finished our wagon train was ordered to cross at Messenger's* [Ferry]. *Drove until one o'clock. Heaviest rain I have ever witnessed and very heavy thunder. Slept in a wagon about half double for want of room. Two men killed.*

Wednesday, July 8, 1863
Head Qarter [sic] *Train. Got to Messenger's ferry* [sic] *at an early hour. Took a good nap and marched on with the train 9 A.C. toward Jackson. Got ahead of the train and spent the night with a teamster of the ammunition train. Felt very tired when we stopped about three o'clock am of Thursday.*

He probably slept under or in one of the ammunition wagons. Why he is not moving with the Headquarters wagon train at this time is not clear.

Thursday, July 9, 1863
Head Quarter [wagon] *Train Near Jackson Miss. Number of horses and mules were poisoned and died from drinking in ponds supposed to have been poisoned by the Rebels.*

About this time the Headquarters wagons went through, and he writes:

Friday, July 10, 1863
Head Quarter [wagon] *Train Two miles from Jackson Miss. Caught up with Head Quarters about dusk and soon spread my blanket. The other boys took supper. Jackson* [Stonewall Jackson] *surrounded on three sides. Water very scarce.*

Saturday, July 11, 1863

Hd. Qrs. 9th A.C. Near Jackson Mississippi. Firing commenced about 7 in the morning. Skirmishing continued all day. Rebel skirmishers in trees fired down on our men in the field. . . . Talked with some negroes who came out from Jackson. Cotton was hauled for breastworks. [Cotton plants were being used to camouflage their positions facing the enemy.]

What are breastworks?

Breastworks are fortifications made of piled material such as logs, fence rails, and stones. They are usually built up to breast height, thus the name *breastworks*. They were often converted to a rampart if they were used long-term. A *rampart* is a length of embankment forming part of a defensive boundary of a fortified site. It is usually broad-topped and made of excavated earth or masonry.

A line of Union Army breastworks (Library of Congress)

Sunday, July 12, 1863

Hd. Qrs. 9th A.C. Near Jackson Miss. Cannonading [bombardment] *commenced about 7 in the morning but did not continue long. No general engagement* [fighting] *during the day. . . . Moved Head Quarters about 5 P.M. and put up our tent. Alarm at night. Rebs reported moving either on our right or excavating. Heard of* [General] *Mead's* [sic] *victory in Penna.*

Tuesday, July 14, 1863

Hd. Qrs. 9th A.C. Near Jackson Miss. A spy who had been among the rebels and all over the state of Mississippi, came to the General's tent in the night under guard. Artillery firing was ordered every five minutes. Flag of truce granted for rebs to bury some of our dead...

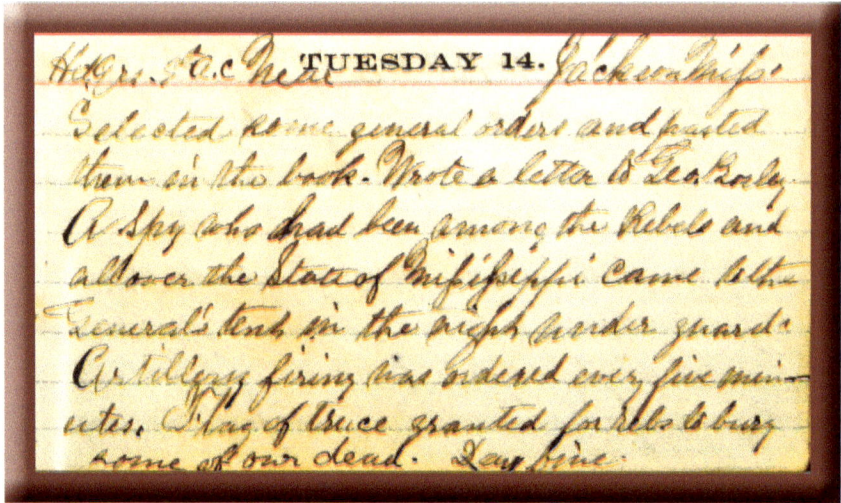

July 14, 1863: Burying our dead

Union army entrenchments in Vicksburg (Library of Congress)

Wednesday, July 15, 1863
Hd. Qrs. 9th A.C. Near Jackson Miss. Were aroused at 5 A.M. by the General and the spy wanting some paper. Received valuable information. Heard that Dix and Keys had taken Richmond. Newspapers give account of [General] Meade's victory in Penna. No general engagement here.

Thursday, July 16, 1863
Head Quarters 9th A.C. Near Jackson Miss. Heavy firing among the skirmishers early in the morning. . . . We are down to half rations of salt and hardtack.

What is hardtack?

Hardtack is made from flour, water, and salt. It was known as *sheet iron crackers* or *tooth duller* because it was so hard. Soldiers really didn't like eating it. It also was prone to absorb moisture, which allowed mold to grow in the boxes that were supplied to the Army. Insects would sometimes lay their eggs in the hardtack, giving it the nickname, *worm castles.*

Hardtack was important for the men to eat because it provided the energy they needed. It was a big part of their diet, so they tried many different ways to eat it. The most common method to soften hardtack was to dunk it in coffee. This was also a way to help kill the little maggots and worms that lived inside of it, allowing soldiers to skim them off of the top of the coffee.

It was not a very appetizing food.

Friday, July 17, 1863
Head Quarters 9th A.C. Near Jackson Miss. First report in the morning - Jackson evacuated. . . . Copied a number of orders and wrote out orders sending a number of men to their regiments again. Col. Bowen ordered us to keep everybody out of the office but those who belong in it.

Saturday, July 18, 1863
Head Quarters 9th A.C. Near Jackson Miss. Our forces engaged in destroying Rail Road. . . . Signal officer was buried about dark. Heard that Fort Sumter and all the batteries on James Island but one were captured by our forces.

Sunday, July 19, 1863
Head Quarters 9th A.C. Near Jackson Miss. 1st Division came back from destroying Rail Road. . . . Got orders to move at three o'clock. . .

Monday, July 20, 1863
Head Qrs. 9th A.C. Near Brownsville Miss. Arose a little after three o'clock, struck the office tent and started on the march about 5 A.M. Rode in an ambulance. . . . Marched 15 miles during the day and spent the night within four miles of Brownsville. Some of the men died after getting into camp.

Wednesday, July 29, 1863
Head Qrs 9th A.C. Milldale Miss. Boys all impatient to go North.

Thursday, July 30, 1863
Hd. Qrs. 9th A.C. Milldale Miss. Number of Citizens came to the General to complain about their property. Could not sleep until after midnight on account of the Mosquito Concert at my head.

Saturday, August 1, 1863
Hd. Qrs. 9th A.C. Milldale Miss. Our sick and wounded 800 in number embarking.

Sunday, August 2, 1863
Head Quarters 9th A.C. Milldale Miss. Went out to the woods in the morning and spent more than an hour in prayer and reading my bible. The 84th Psalm had a peculiar sweetness, one father read at family worship before I left home on the 28th Oct. 1861.

About this time he becomes ill with dysentery. His entries day after day just say he is "unwell." Meanwhile he is trying to carry on his duties at Headquarters Company. Finally an entry says:

Saturday August 7, 1863
Hd. Qrs. 9th A.C. On Board Jno. H. Groesbeck Left Milldale about half past three in the afternoon and got on board the Groesbeck.

Saturday, August 8, 1863
Hd. Qrs. 9th A.C. (Groesbeck) Vicksburg Miss. Landed at V [Vicksburg] about 2 o'clock. Went on shore at daylight and took a walk through the city. Was very much disappointed in its appearance. Not so much destroyed as I supposed. Crossed over to the Louisiana side at three o'clock P.M. and took on coal. Crossed back at one and started up the river at two in the morning.

Monday, August 10, 1863
Hd. Qrs. 9th A.C. On Board John H. Groesbeck. Landed near the mouth of the White river and took a soldier on board from a gunboat, who was very badly burned. Took a dose of Morphine before going to bed.

Thursday, August 13, 1863
Hd Qrs. 9th AC. On Board Jno. H Groesbeck. Boat seemed to run very slow. . . . Felt much better than I had done for some days.

August 1, 1863: 800 men sick or wounded

Friday, August 14, 1863
Hd. Qrs. 9th A.C. On Board the Groesbeck Landed at Columbus Ky. in the morning and Brig. Gen. Smith & staff got off. Landed at Cairo about noon. Major General Jno G. Parke & staff took the cars [train] *and left us on the boat. Doctor left quite a number of sick men without proper care.*

Saturday, August 15, 1863
Cairo Ill. Hd Qrs. 9th. A. C. Commenced unloading the boat early in the morning. . . . Heard Major General Jno A Logan speak a few minutes. Did not wait to hear him through. Waited until midnight for our car.

    He was becoming ill frequently, and his entries indicate that the problem was interfering with his work.

Sunday, September 13, 1863
Hd. Qrs. 9th A.C. Lexington Ky.
Was too unwell to attend church. took some powders during the day but they did not seem to do much good. Felt very weak.

Monday, September 14, 1863
Hd. Qrs. 9th A.C. Lexington Ky. Was extremely unwell all day. Did not work much in the office although there was a large pile of printed orders to distribute.

Tuesday, September 15, 1863
Hd. Qrs. 9th A.C. Lexington Ky. My health was some better during the day. Taking prepared arsenic, and quinine.

    Finally the army doctor gave him a furlough to go home "for a spell" to rest and get well.

Thursday, September 17, 1863
Soldier's Home Cincinnati, O. Got orders to pack up . . . arrived at Cincinnati about eight.

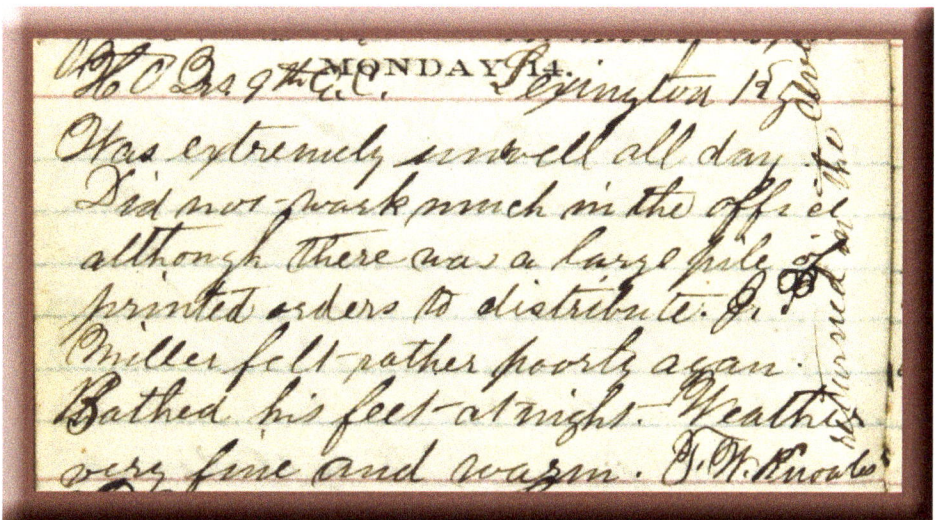

September 14, 1863: *"Was extremely unwell all day."*

Saturday, September 19, 1863
Home. Left Cincinnati at 11 oc in the evening previous. At Columbus at daylight and changed cars. Got to Steubenville at 12-30. Hired horses and carriage. Took rest at Mr. Miller's. Got home about 5 o'clock. Folks just done supper. Very much surprised.

   He is still home at the end of 1863. There are no special entries. The war is still raging; and he celebrates Thanksgiving, Christmas, and New Year's quietly at home.

Clerks at the Provost Marshall HQ near Fredericksburg, Virginia, circa 1863. (Library of Congress)

1864: More Health Problems, Then Back to the War

Late in 1863 Samuel got a certificate from a civilian Dr. Scott saying that he was fit to return to military duty. So, with the certificate and some medicine prescribed by Dr. Scott, he prepares to return to military life.

Monday, January 11, 1864
At Home. Changed my citizen's for soldier's clothes. Weather very cold.

Tuesday, January 12, 1864
Steubenville Ohio. Went to Mr. Cassidy's and bade them farewell. Left home about 12½ o'clock. Crossed the river [Ohio River] in a skiff. Bought Diaries, paper, pen, envelopes, etc. Went to depot. Spent the night very pleasantly at McConnel's [Mills].

Thursday, January 14, 1864
Columbus Ohio. Reported at hospital & was sent to Provost Marshal. . . . Sent back to barracks. Left Columbus on the 10 OC [o'clock] train. Large train filled with soldiers. Two of our number in irons as deserters.

Friday, January 22, 1864
General Hospital, Lexington Ky. Arose in Exchange Barracks at Louisville at 3-45, took breakfast, started on the train at 5½, and reached Lexington at 11 o'clock. Reported to Provost Marshal, sent to Barracks No. 1. Went to Head Quarters, thence to hospital & was examined, sent back to Head Quarters & received into hospital. Slept on the floor.

Now, from January 22 to February 9, 1864, he was assigned to the hospital, writing letters for the men and helping to care for them.

Thursday, January 28, 1864
General Hospital, Lexington Kentucky. Read a little book entitled "The Soldier's Pocketbook." . . . Procured a pass and visited the cemetery in the afternoon. Felt the necessity of a closer walk with God. Communion with him seemed sweet, and reading his word a delightful duty.

Wednesday, February 3, 1864
General Hospital, Lexington Kentucky. My 25th birthday. Spent part of the forenoon attending the sick. Read some in Bunyan's Pilgrim's Progress.

Wednesday, February 10, 1864
Provost Marshal's Office Lexington Ky. Was sent to the Provost Marshal's office as clerk and moved my things thither. Slept on a rather poor bed.

He makes no negative comment about sleeping on the floor in any of his entries, but when he gets a bunk or cot in the Provost Marshall's office and quarters, he notes that he is sleeping on a "poor bed."

Saturday, February 13, 1864
Office of Provost Marshal Lexington Ky. Two boys about 16 years old in the office trying to get home. Intended to enlist as teamsters but the man whom they went with disappointed them and left them to get home the best way they could.

Sunday, February 14, 1864
Office of Provost Marshal Lexington Ky. Two officers were arrested drunk in Broadway Hotel and brought to the office, quite noisy and bleeding.

Sunday, February 21, 1864
Office of Provost Marshal Lexington Ky. Took breakfast at the hospital at the usual hour. Had mush, cornbread and beef soup for breakfast. No wheat bread.

Monday, February 22, 1864
Office of Provost Marshal, Lexington, Ky. Made out the Morning Report. Rec'd 73 Deserters, Convalescents, and Recruits about noon, and having rolls to make out I was not able to attend church in the evening.

Friday, February 26, 1864
Office of Provost Marshal Lexington Ky. Made out the morning report, and spent most of the forenoon making out lists of men to be sent off. [He does not say who, why or where.] *Capt. Park confiscated seven barrels of whiskey in one house.*

Tuesday, March 1, 1864
Office of Provost Marshal Lexington Ky. Two women, Refugees from Tennessee came in in the morning and were furnished with quarters after some delay.

Thursday, March 3, 1864
Office of Provost Marshal Lexington Ky. Were paid off in the forenoon. Received six months pay and my clothing account was settled up to Oct. 31st. Sent home $100. . . . Family of refugees came in. Capt. Park seemed to care but little for them.

Monday, March 7, 1864
Office of Provost Marshal Lexington Ky. Colby let a spy escape from custody by going to supper.

   Now this is strange. A man is ordered to guard a spy but he goes to supper instead, and the spy escapes. There is no mention of what happened to the soldier who would rather eat than guard a spy.

Saturday, March 12, 1864
Office of Provost Marshal Lexington Ky. Made out some lists in the morning which did not exactly please Capt. Park and he made them out again.

Tuesday, March 15, 1864
Office of Provost Marshal Lexington Ky. Two men were arrested in the evening as deserters from Camp Nelson. Did not retire until after midnight.

Friday, March 18, 1864
Office of Provost Marshal Lexington Ky. A woman with two little children came in late, refugees, and I gave them my bed and slept on a bench.

Wednesday, March 30, 1864
Office of Provost Marshal Lexington Ky. Received my discharge from the hospital.

He was reporting to the hospital at least once a day while assigned to the Provost Marshal's office in Lexington, Kentucky. Now he's hoping to get back to the Headquarters Company. He evidently has orders to do so, and he begins the journey.

Thursday, March 31, 1864
Office of Provost Marshal Lexington Ky. Finished the monthly report and got my transportation to Covington [Kentucky]. *Left Lexington at 1-10 with Lt. Hubbell. Went over into Cincinnati & reported at Hd. Qrs. and then returned to the barracks. . . . Slept on a bunk without any straw. . . . Troops coming in from the front.*

He is now in a place called Covington Barracks. He stayed at Covington Barracks a few days with no particular assignment, then he is ordered on board a river steamer called the *Revenue*.

Wednesday, April 6, 1864
Hurricane Deck Steamer Revenue. Left Covington Barracks at one and at two o'clock left Covington and started up river. Boat heavily ladened. [The hurricane deck is the upper deck on a passenger steamship.]

Friday, April 8, 1864
Hurricane Deck Steamer "Revenue." Reached Parkersburg at 10½ o'clock. Were not permitted to go ashore. Slept on Hurricane Deck. Rained hard in the night but we were pretty well covered with rubber blankets.

Thursday, April 14, 1864
Annapolis M. @ Depot 9th A.C. Found the clerks in the morning in the office. Ate breakfast with the Hd. Qr. Guards. . . . Streets awful muddy. Soldier shot in the streets by an officer.

Wednesday, April 20, 1864
Hd. Qrs. Co. A. 100th P.V.V. near Annapolis Md. Spent most of the day in making up old accounts for Capt. Pentecost, footed up accounts in the evening & found that they did not check correctly. . . . Some rumors of a move.

Saturday, April 23, 1864
Camp 100th P.V.V. Between Annapolis Md. & Washington D.C. Broke Camp at six o'clock. Left Annapolis about 9 OC.

The next few days are spent marching and sleeping. Samuel falls behind the regiment at times due to his feet "giving out." It is a tough journey.

Thursday, April 28, 1864
Camp 100th P.V.V. Bristol Station Va. Had orders to be ready to move at six o'clock in the morning. Packed up, and, the morning being very cold, gathered around the fires. Moved at eight o'clock. Marching was more regular than the day previous. Went into camp about half past six P.M.

This would seem to be a 10-hour march at a regular pace, not a forced march.

Saturday, April 30, 1864
Camp 100th Pa. Vet. Vols. Bealton Station Va. Got orders to pack up. Was detailed as clerk at Hd Qrs. 2nd Brig. 1st Division 9th A. C. [artillery company] *before leaving Warrenton.*

Tuesday, May 3, 1864
Hd. Qrs. 2nd Brig. 1st Div. 9th A.C. Bealeton Va. Spent the day at Head Quarters writing out orders. Got the books squared up.

He now seems to be fairly well set in his assignment as a Headquarters Company clerk—as firm as one can get in a wartime condition, but:

Wednesday, May 4, 1864
Camp 100th P.V.V. near Germanna Ford Va. Packed up in the morning about six o'clock and were soon on the march. Put my knapsack in the Brigade Hd. Qr. Wagon and carried only a blanket and my rations. [Putting his knapsack in the Brigade wagon was a mark of belonging. Even though he is considered a clerk, he can pull guard and combat duty.]

Thursday, May 5, 1864

Camp 100th P.V.V. Near Germanna Ford Va. Marched about two miles in the morning and stacked arms as reserve for the Army of the Potomac. About 1½ o'clock we heard the first firing. Remained in that position until night when we went about two miles on picket.

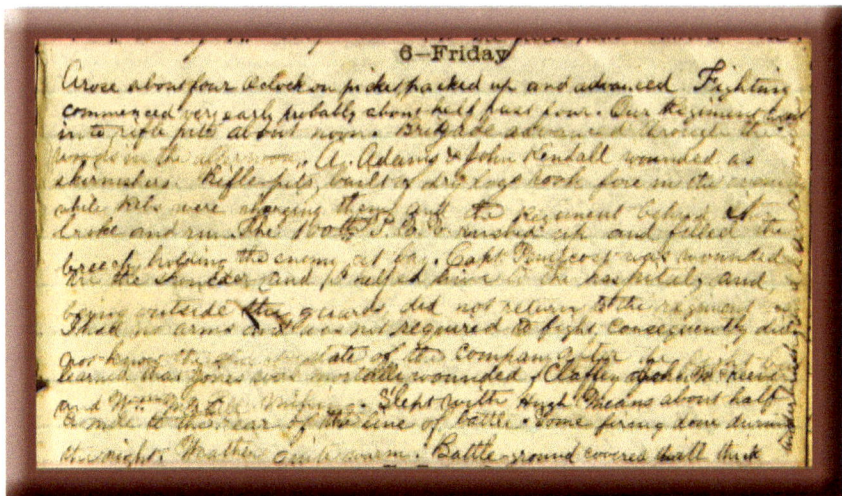

May 6, 1864: The *Battle of the Wilderness* begins.
It was a huge and costly battle.

The next few entries contain Samuel's account of what became known as *The Battle of the Wilderness*. This was the first battle of General Grant's Virginia Overland Campaign against General Lee. It is considered one of the Civil War's decisive battles. More than 3,500 lives were lost over these few days.

Friday, May 6, 1864

Hd. Qrs. 2nd Brigade 1st Div. Artillery Company in the field near Chancelorsville [sic]. Arose about four o'clock on picket, packed up and advanced. Fighting commenced very early probably about half past four. Our Regiment went into rifle pits about noon. Brigade advanced through the woods in the afternoon. A. Adams & John Kendall wounded as skirmishers. Rifle pits, built of dry logs, took fire in the evening while Rebs were charging them and the regiment behind it broke and ran. The 100th PVV rushed up and filled the breech, holding the

Captain Pentecost

Battle of the Wilderness (Library of Congress)

enemy at bay. Capt. Pentecost was wounded in the shoulder, and I helped him to the hospital, and being outside the guards did not return to the regiment as I had no arms and was not required to fight. Consequently did not know the exact state of the company after the fight, but learned that Jones was mortally wounded, Claffey, John McKeever and Wm. Magill missing. . . . Battle ground covered with thick underbrush and leaves on fire.

Saturday, May 7, 1864
Hd. Qrs. 2nd Brig. 1st Div. 9th A.C. In the Field. No fighting on our line. Heavy fighting on our right and left. Negroes reported to have fought bravely and taken a brigade of Reb prisoners. Lee's left flank reported turned and he retreating. Slept by our guns, what little we slept before marching. One volley fired upon our own Sharp Shooters in mistake after dark as they came out of the woods.

Sunday, May 8 , 1864
Head Qrs 2 Brig 1st Div. 9th A.C. Near Chancelorville [sic] Va. About one o'clock A.M. we were aroused from our slumbers near the rifle pits and started toward Fredericksburg. Marched until 3 A.M., then slept until 6½. Burnside Reported along the line, Fort Darling captured by Smith and Butler. Went into camp about 3 P.M. . . . Slept but little during the night awaiting orders to move. Our division not engaged during the day.

Monday, May 9, 1864

Hd Qrs 2nd Brig. 1st Div. 9th A.C. Nie Run Va. Left camp at three o'clock in the morning and marched until noon. Got off our way and had to march about two miles extra. Regiment throwing up breast works in the afternoon. Very heavy firing on our right about dark. Gen'l Sedgwick killed in the evening. Reb Gen'l Longstreet reported captured, and Reb Gen'l Stevens killed. Slept well during the night although in suspense. Feared for the termination of the battle as our right seemed to be giving back. Some fighting during the night and Rebels driven 1½ miles by Gen'l Meade's forces.

Tuesday, May 10, 1864

Hd Qrs 1st Div 9th A.C. Nie Run Va. Brig. Gen'l T.G. Stevenson killed by an almost spent ball about 8½ o'clock in the morning. Ball passed through a canteen and hit him in the head whilst he was eating his breakfast under an apple tree. Col. Leasure took command of first Division. Our Brigade engaged in throwing up rifle pits. At six o'clock P.M. our forces advanced and drove the Rebs about a mile without loss to us. Was on the hill with Hd Qr horses and saw the advance. Horses afterward ordered forward. Our left wing thrown forward toward Spotsylvania Court House. Rebs reported flanked on both right and left. Some skirmishing done during the night, and Division Head Qrs fell back to the position occupied in the evening to be out of range of shot. Slept from about 12 o'clock until morning, being disturbed only once by a volley being fired along the line.

Colonel Daniel Leasure

Wednesday, May 11, 1864

Hd Qrs 1st Div 9th A.C. Nie Run Va. Everything seemed to be quiet during the day except an occasional shot fired. About four o'clock our Div. left their rifle pits and recrossed the stream leaving the grounds at the disposal of the enemy. Our troops being re-formed, returned to their position. Some cannonading in the evening. Very heavy rain between five & six o'clock. After taking supper our mess put up some shelter on poles and kindled large fire to dry the ground. Did not know exactly where Col. Leasure and staff were. Gen'l Burnside's clerks came into the edge of the woods where we were. Slept very comfortably during the night Cannonading kept up occasionally.

Thursday, May 12, 1864

Wagon Train Hd Qrs 2nd Brig 1st Div. 9th A.C. Near Fredericksburg Va. Met with the boys of Corps Head Quarters in the morning & took breakfast with them. . . . Started to go to the Brigade, but was cut off by the enemy's artillery fire. . . . Severe fighting all day seemingly all along the lines. Gen'l Burnside reported along the lines, "7,000 prisoners & 15 pieces of artillery captured." Saw quite a number of them under guard among whom was Brig. Gen'l Stewart. 100th P.V.V. engaged in the forenoon and occasionally during the afternoon. . . . Several men killed. Two brothers in one company, standing side by side, were wounded with one bullet, one in the right arm and the other in the left.

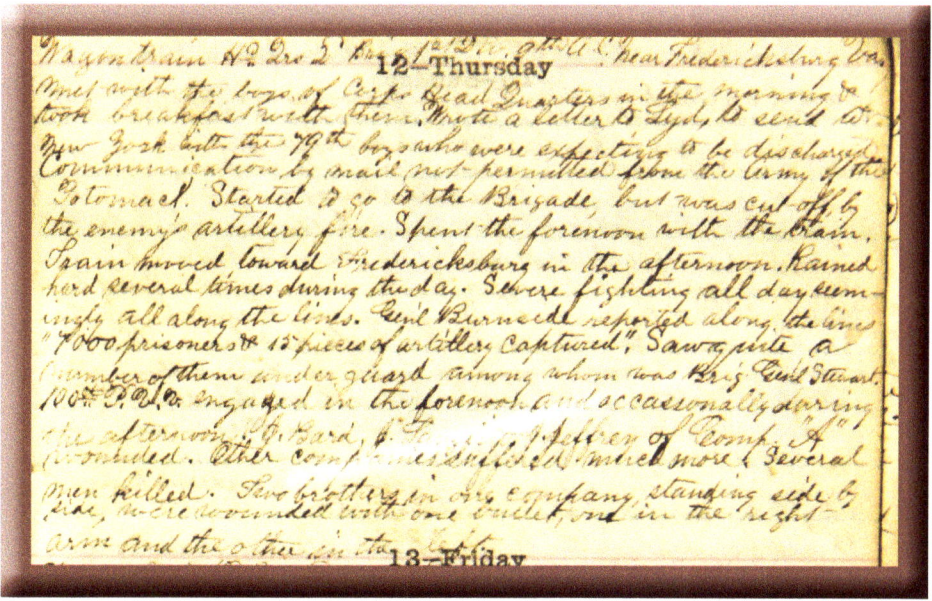

May 12, 1864: 7,000 prisoners and 15 pieces of artillery captured

Friday, May 13, 1864

Wagon Train Hd. Qrs. 2nd Brig 1st Div 9th A.C. Near Fredericksburg Va. Arose about six o'clock and took breakfast with the Commissary's clerks. Some of the boys from our regiment came by who were wounded. Helped to dress one of their wounds. Col. Leasure came in sick and unable to command his Brigade. . . . Great number of prisoners passed in the morning. . . . Butchers reported quite a number of wounded lying outside of our hospital in the rain with their wounds undressed. Read, and studied upon the 1st and 2nd chapters of Hebrews in the evening. Felt the need of a closer walk with God.

Saturday, May 14, 1864
Wagon Train Hd Qrs 2nd Brig 1st Div. 9th A.C. Near Fredericksburg Va. Was very comfortably situated while many of my comrades were suffering with wet and hunger. Heard that John Langfitt had his leg taken off from the effect of a wound received from a Sharp Shooter's rifle. 4,000 of our prisoners reported recaptured by our cavalry and taken to Gen'l Butler. News rather too good to be true. Richmond reported captured by Butler. Uncertain.

Sunday, May 15, 1864
Wagon Train 2nd Brig. 1st Div 9th A.C. Near Fredricksburg, Va. Went to the front about nine miles on horseback for Col. Leasure's Certificate of Disability. Started twenty five minutes before nine and returned twenty five minutes past two. While at Gen'l Burnside's Hd Qrs the enemy threw some shells over our heads. Saw the 140th Pa. Vols and had a short conversation with some of my acquaintances. Found them all well. . . . Did not see the 100th P.V.V's nor hear any word from them. Learned in the evening that our Corps occupied the extreme right of our line, and the wagon train being exposed to the enemy, was ordered to be ready to move toward Fredericksburg at six in the morning. Rained very hard in the evening. Roads almost impassable.

Union Army wagon train crossing the Rapahannock River near Fredericksburg
(Library of Congress)

Monday, May 16, 1864

Hd Qr, Wagon Train 1st Div. 9th A.C. Fredericksburg. Packed up in the morning and moved the train about two miles nearer Fredericksburg to get into a more safe position. Got into camp about 11½ o'clock. Pitched our tents and made ourselves comfortable. Col. Leasure went to the hospital, some of the boys caught some very nice fish. . . . James Pomeroy came from the front and reported all things quiet. Came to the train for provisions. We were almost out of rations. . . . Rained some during the day. Roads very muddy.

Tuesday, May 17, 1864

Wagon Train 1st Div. 9th A.C. Near Fredericksburg Va. About 9½ oclock A.M. the Order came "Pack up." Soon tents were struck and everything in the wagons. [Think about these moves. Desks, chairs, tables, files, supplies, tents, kitchen tents—everything had to be loaded by hand on the horse- or mule-drawn wagons and then unloaded and set up again at their new destination.] *Moved towards Fredericksburg. Surveyed the heights on which the Rebs fought us in 1862. Awful strong fortifications, and took but little work to build them. Moved on to the hill on the Spotsylvania turnpike and went into camp about noon. . . . Very near out of rations and no Commissary with us to draw from. Lieuts Morrison & Weller went to town*

One of the grim realities of war is that people die. During the Civil war, approximately 620,000 soldiers died, making it the deadliest conflict in U.S. history. This photo shows the burial of Union soldiers on May 19, 1864, within Reb lines under a flag of truce. (Library of Congress)

and bought some rations, Coffee Sugar and fresh beef. Number of the boys begging "Hard Tack." One fellow begged a cracker of us for the men of the 3rd Maryland. Gave him four.

Thursday, May 19, 1864
Wagon Train 1st Div, 9th A.C. Near Fredericksburg Va. About 7½ o'clock we received the intelligence that the Rebs had attacked Lieut. Justice's supply train, and had killed some of the drivers and horses. Soon we received orders to pack up and moved back about a mile toward Fredericksburg. Got into camp again about eleven o'clock and pitched our tents. Considerable of anxiety felt concerning the train.

Friday, May 20, 1864
Wagon Train 1st Div. 9th A.C. Near Fredericksburg Va. About noon we got orders to pack up. Train moved into the city in the afternoon and went into camp. Lieut. Justice came to us in the evening and gave us a history of Thursday's fight at the supply train. About fifteen hundred men killed and wounded. Three hundred killed. [He does not say whether these are Union or Confederate soldiers. The siege of Fredericksburg is evidently over, and they are moving in to occupy the city.] *Rebels did not succeed in getting anything away with them. Had they struck the road a little nearer Fredericksburg, they could have taken the train, but they struck too near our right flank and were repulsed. Quartermaster brought us some rations from the front. Men seemed to be lying in comparative ease and comfort. Fredericksburg has once been a fine & pleasant little city. Beautiful scenery around the city. Cemetery on the west side. Mrs. Washington's grave northwest of the city.*

We can assume that he is referring to Mrs. George Washington's grave here.

Sunday, May 22, 1864
Wagon Train on the road between Fredericksburg and Bowling Green. About one o'clock Applebee, driving the hospital team, upset his wagon in a mud hole. Was not got out until 9 o'clock. Great many things spoiled by the water. . . . Moved very slowly on account of the great number of wagons on the road. Almost all the teams of the Army of the Potomac in the vicinity. Heard some cannonading during the day but heard nothing from the fight.

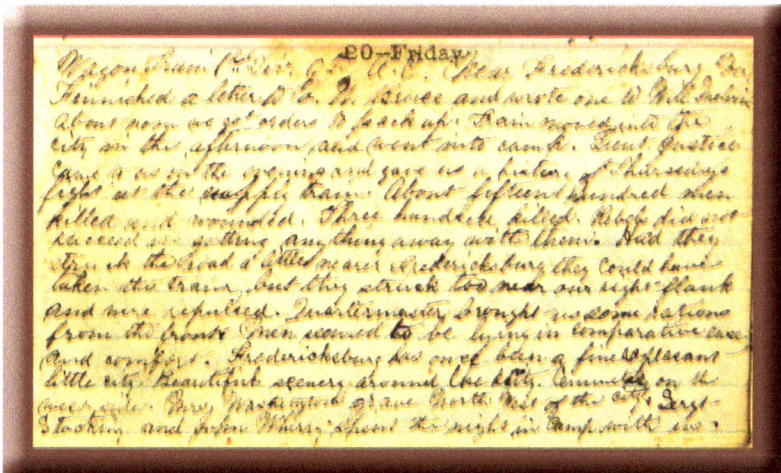
May 20, 1864: 1,500 men killed or wounded

Saturday, May 28, 1864
Wagon Train 1st Division, 9th A.C. near Newtown, Va. Arose at 4 o'clock and found some cavalry men attempting to take some of our horses. Harnessed up and were soon on the road to Corell. . . . Heard that Gen'l Lee had proposed to surrender Richmond provided Gen'l Grant would not destroy it.

Tuesday, May 31, 1864
Wagon Train 1st Division, 9th A.C. near New Castle, Va. Report from the front that Gen'l Lee was either killed or mortally wounded. [This report proved to be false, but it illustrates that the dissemination of information in those days was not always accurate.]

Thursday, June 2, 1864
Wagon Train 1st Division, 9th A.C. Very heavy firing heard during the day. Report that Lee sent in a flag of truce asking for four hours in which to bury his dead & Grant replied that he would give him, in lieu thereof, four hours of the hardest fighting he ever did, and it was so.

Friday, June 3, 1864
Wagon Train 1st Div. 9th A.C. Near Cold Harbor Va. Learned that our regiment had suffered severely in yesterday's fight. Lost about 90 men killed, wounded and missing. Jacob McCullough killed and Nelson wounded with some others of Co. A. . . . Quarter Master Justice's supply train was attacked by guerrillas. One man killed and eighteen horses taken from the train. . . . Great number of wounded men passed our camp in the evening, and some prisoners.

Sunday, June 5, 1864
Wagon Train 1st Div,. 9th A.C. Near Cold Harbor. At ten minutes before nine o'clock P.M. very heavy cannonading and musketry commenced seemingly but a short distance from our camp, and continued about half an hour. Was kept up at intervals during the night. One citizen teamster had his horse saddled ready to leave the train provided the rebels should come in.

Tuesday, June 7, 1864
Wagon Train 1st Div. 9th A.C. Near Cold Harbor Va. Could not hear much firing during the day. Heard a heavy gun occasionally. Number of citizen drivers discharged and sent home. Soldiers detailed in their places. Got clear of the team which I had been driving. Weather was very fine and warm. Roads dusty and the sand made the roads difficult to travel over. Rather unwell during the day and evening.

Wednesday, June 8, 1864
Wagon Train 1st Div. 9th A.C. Near Cold Harbor Va. A number of Rebel Prisoners were taken past our quarters. Firing was kept up during the day and became more incessant in the evening. . . . Felt unwell during the day. Got some camphor and opium pills from S. Norgrave, who came to the wagon train from medical stores. . . . General Crittenden was relieved from the command of the 1st Div. & General Ludly took his place.

Thursday, June 9, 1864
Wagon Train 1st Div. 9th A.C. White house Landing Va. Great many teams with only two horses. Teams of our regiment got along very well. 3rd Maryland teams fell behind. . . . Met Maj. Gen'l Jno. G. Park. Reported that our army was changing base of operations to Harrison's Landing. Our camp was established in a fine clover meadow. Horses turned loose to graze. Good water. Camp presents very fine appearance, and quite a number of boats at the wharf. Was quite unwell during the day with Diarrhea.

Friday, June 10, 1864
Commissary 2nd Brig 1st Div 9th A.C. Near Cold Harbor Va. Lieut. Morrison asked me to go to the front with forage [food for the horses] *for the Brigade and I consented. Started about four o'clock & had to wait on the road until half past five before we got started fairly on the road waiting for an escort from which we ran away as soon as we got the chance and left the rest of the train. . . . Report in the afternoon that Genl Butler had captured Fort Darling and four thousand prisoners.*

Saturday, June 11, 1864
White House Landing Va. Wagon Train 2nd Brig 1st Div 9th A.C. Traveled with a Lieutenant of the 44th New York who had been captured by the Rebels and recaptured by Sherridan's [sic] cavalry. He was a very pleasant comrade. We took dinner of Hard Tack & Coffee together.

Sunday, June 12, 1864
Hd. Qrs. 2nd Brig. 1st Div. 9th A.C. Near White House Landing Va. Received orders to move with the Brigade Head Quarters wagon. John J Book driving. Had orders to be ready to move about six o'clock and moved about eight toward the White House Landing. . . . Troops very tired and many of them unwell. Was quite unwell myself. Drove some during the night.

Monday, June 13, 1864
Head Qrs. 2nd Brig. 1st Div. 9th A.C. Near Chickahominy River, Va. After marching all night we went to a field near White house [sic] landing and there rested until noon, we then started toward the James River. Marched until half past eleven o'clock when we went into camp. Stopped about 6 o'clock and had coffee. Seemed to march as though we were running Gen'l Lee a race to the James River. Bought a paper after dark and read it by candlelight. No very especial news in it, but all encouraging. Stood the days march much better than I have stood some other marches. . . . Felt very much disgusted with the actions of some of the 3 Maryland officers, who got into the H. Qr wagon and rode up hill and down. They had Whiskey on the wagon with them and used it freely.

Tuesday, June 14, 1864
Hd Qrs. 2nd Brig. 1st Div. 9th A.C. Near James River Va. Arose about half past four o'clock and marched until noon when we stopped in a large bottom after crossing the Chickahominy River, drew beef and took dinner. Did not have time to get the beef more than half cooked until we were ordered to move. Stopped about five o'clock and took supper. Got into camp about eight, and after we had the horses unhitched and unharnessed and the men were nearly all asleep we were ordered to move about three hundred yards across . . . to connect our brigade with Gen'l Potter's. Consequently we were obliged to obey. Gen'l Potter was so drunk during the afternoon that, while our brigade was resting beside the road, he inquired, "What men are all these here?" Was very much disgusted with the management of affairs and with drunken officers. Our rations were running very low, and no Brigade Commissary along and no way of getting rations.

Thursday, June 16, 1864

Hd Qrs 2nd Brig. 1st Div. 9th A.C. Near Petersburg, Va. Crossed the pontoon bridge across the James River near Charles City at half past one o'clock A.M. and marched until 9 when we stopped an hour, took breakfast and marched until five in the evening, and as soon as our corps was in position a fight was commenced. . . . a shell or solid shot cut the top from a tree near by, and in falling it brushed my head. When we got things arranged, I laid me down and slept, being very tired, notwithstanding fighting was kept up all night. . . . Four forts captured during the evening and several guns. Our brigade was not called into action, although some of its members were wounded. Weather very warm and dry and the roads very dusty.

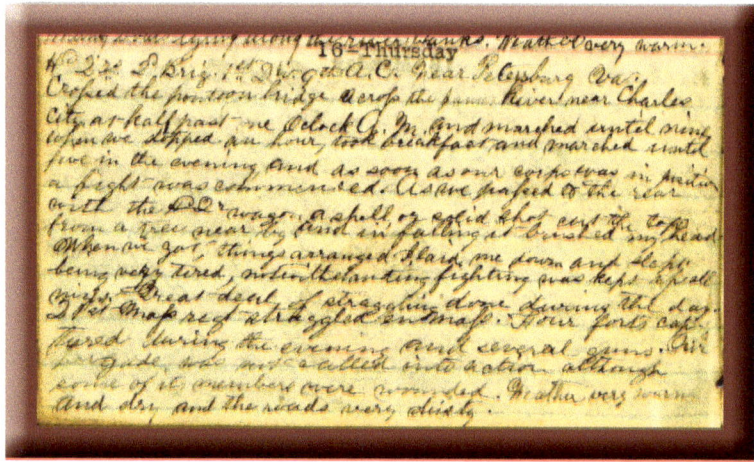

June 16, 1864: "shell . . . cut the top from a tree . . . it brushed my head"

Friday, June 17, 1864

Hd Qrs. 2nd Brig 1st Div. 9th A.C. Near Petersburg Va. Comparative quiet was maintained on our immediate front during the forenoon. In the evening our brigade made a charge on the enemy's works and took them, but ran out of ammunition and were obliged to leave them. The 100th Regiment were thrown forward as skirmishers and after ward formed part of the line of battle. Comp. "A" lost two killed and nine wounded. Billy Gray & John Clemmons killed. Couboy, Pale, France, J. Magill, Mullen, McFarland, Clarke, Kerrens & S. Fowler wounded. Lt. Colonel Dawson was severely wounded in the shoulder. Capt. Morrow of Co. "H" killed. Wrote a letter to R.S. Criss and commenced one to father and mother. Spent the evening on the hill watching for the charge. Gen'l. Ludly Comdg our division and his aids were said to have been very drunk during the charge. Gen'l Potter was also drunk and made a charge sometime during the day.

Saturday, June, 18, 1864

Hd Qrs. 2nd Brig. 1st Div 9th A.C. Near Petersburg Va. Felt very unwell during the day and did not visit the hospital until evening. Such a sight, I never before beheld so many and such various wounds. Some one [sic] had stolen a watch and hat from Alex Kerns while he was under the influence of Chloriform [sic] to have his arm amputated. Found Colonel Dawson suffering severely from his wound. Moved our quarters about a half a mile to the front in the evening.

Sunday, June 19, 1864

Hd Qrs 2nd Brig 1st Div. 9th A.C. Near Petersburg Va. Were ordered toward the front in the evening. Jim Barr and I took a walk over the battle ground where our company fought on the 17th where Billy Grey and John Clemmens were killed. Saw quite a number of graves, and piles of Rebels buried in their rifle pits. Ground almost covered with rifle pits which our men dug to protect themselves in. At half past ten Oclock P.M. there was some tolerably heavy fighting but it did not last long. Visited Company A and found the boys in pretty good spirits although only able to stack twenty guns, non commissioned officers and all.

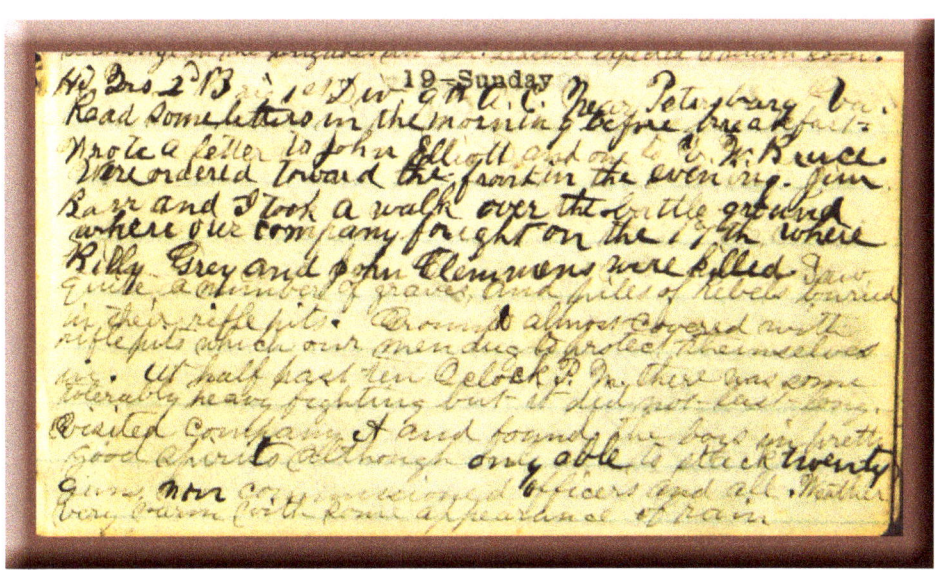

June 19, 1864: Walking the battlefield where Samuel's friends Billy Grey and John Clemmens were killed.

Monday, June 20, 1864
Hd Qrs. 2nd Brig 1st Div 9th A.C, Near Petersburg Va. Spent the day in the woods, or rather in the rifle pits near the edge of a wood. . . . At noon we had orders to be ready to move at a moment's warning, and packed the load for that purpose. Our team [horses] *was exchanged for another and better one driven by Hi. Saddler. Had orders at six o'clock to hook up and the brigade moved, but we did not. . . . Picket firing was kept up during the night. Drew rations in the evening and with the rest two days ration of whiskey. I did not draw mine. Some of the boys got boozy. Capt. Clark, A.A.A.G. remarked that if he should see an officer under his command drinking whiskey going into action, he would have him cashiered.* ["Cashiered" means to officially dismiss a person from a military organization, with loss of honor.] *Seemed to think that whiskey was injuring our army. His head all right on that account.*

Saturday, June 25, 1864
Hd Qrs 2nd Brig 1st Div 9th A.C, Near Petersburg, Va. When pickets were being relieved about ten o'clock there was very heavy musketry and again between eleven and twelve. Did not sleep much on account of bullets whistling over our position. Did not take my blanket from my knapsack.

Tuesday, June 28, 1864
Comp A 100th Regt P.V.V. Near Petersburg Va. A brisk picket firing was kept up all night. Shells from different mortars passing to and fro formed a beautiful scene, although doubtless unpleasant to those who were in the vicinity where they bursted [sic]. *. . . Thought considerable about the uncertainty of life and the possibility of death especially under such circumstances as those which surround us at present.*

Sunday, July 3, 1864
Cook's Quarters Comp. "A" 100th P.V.V. Near Petersburg Va. Went to Corps Head Quarters in the evening . . . Everything was remarkably quiet along our lines until late in the evening when picket firing and cannonading was commenced and carried on briskly the greater portion of the night. News of Secretary Chase's resignation in the daily papers. [Treasury Secretary Salmon P. Chase submitted his fourth letter of resignation, and this time President Abraham Lincoln surprised him by accepting it.] *. . . Was said that Gen'l Lee had promised to astonish the world on the fourth and we looked forward with anxiety to the dawning of the day.*

Monday, July 4, 1864
Cooks Quarters Co. "A" 100th P.V.V. Near Petersburg Va. No startling news. Everything remarkably quiet until evening, not averaging perhaps a shot every half hour. In the evening the usual amount of picket firing and mortar shelling was resumed and kept up during the night. Pitched my tent and put up a small bunk upon which I slept very comfortably.

Saturday, July 9, 1864
Cooks Quarters Co. "A" 100th P.V.V. Near Petersburg Va. Walked out in the evening over the forts to view the city of Petersburg. Could only see some of the spires. Felt rather unwell and did not rest well during the night. Disease Diarrhea.

Sunday, July 10, 1864
Cooks Quarters Co. "A" 100th P.V.V. Near Petersburg Va. Michael Currin having procured a pass to go for water, went to the suttlers, bought whiskey, got drunk and used the most abusive language to, and concerning the Capt. for which his hand were tied and a stick run through under his legs and over his arms, the punishment being called "Bucking."

About this time the periodic rifle fire and shelling continues, particularly in the evening. He seems to tolerate the situation pretty well. But on July 11 we read:

Monday, July 11, 1864
Cooks Quarters, Co. "A" 100th P.V.V. Near Petersburg Va. Spent the day in my tent so very unwell that l was unable to move about much, my whole system very much debilitated.

Tuesday, July 12, 1864
Cooks Quarters, Co. A 100th P.V.V. Near Petersburg Va. Was so unwell that I could scarcely carry a canteen of water from the spring. Did not eat anything scarcely during the day. Intended to have written a letter home, but could not. The regiment moved to the front about dark.

Thursday, July 14, 1864

Cooks Quarters, Co. "A" 100th P.V.V. Near Petersburg Va. An order was issued from Corps Head quarters [sic] *detailing me as a clerk somewhere in the 4th Division (colored), but as the Capt. was opposed to having me detailed he had the order revoked. Some idea may be formed of my strength, when it took all that I could muster now to write this so well as it is written.*

Friday, July 15, 1864

Cook's Quarters Co. "A" 100th P.V.V. Near Petersburg Va. Spent the day as days previous were spent without being able to read or write much. . . . Suffered severely all night.

Saturday, July 16, 1864

Cook's Quarters Co. A 100th P.V.V. Near Petersburg Va. Miller visited me and reported my case to Dr. Luddington who said that he would see that ambulance was sent for me by Dr. Mass.

Sunday, July 17, 1864

Field Hospital 1st Div. 9th A.C. Near Petersburg, Va. Told Capt. Pentecost that I must go to to [sic] *the hospital. About three o'clock the ambulance came and I was soon there and very much disappointed with the treatment. Received no medicine as I expected to have received.*

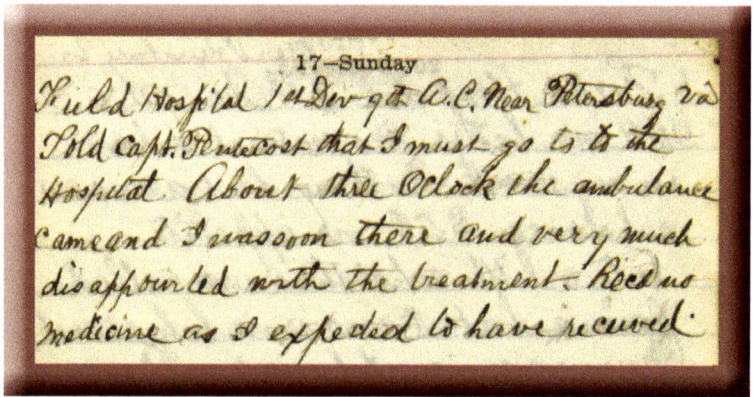

July 17, 1864: Samuel is once again sick and "unwell."

    We don't know exactly what is happening here. He was evidently sick enough to keep him flat on his back. He comments that he cannot move without assistance. He is given whiskey and quinine, but he cannot keep it down. He can't eat or drink without vomiting. Evidently his condition worsens because this entry occurs on July 22, 1864:

Thursday, July 22, 1864
City Point Hospital. Left 1st Division 9 A.C. Hospital about 9½ o'clock. Left my two pieces of shelter tent and my spoon which I could get. Bed at City Point consisted of a tick without filling and my blanket on an iron bedstead.

Saturday, July 23, 1864
City Point Hospital. Was moved to another ward in the evening where I got a good bed. Changed my under clothes and the nurses said my shirt was lousy [infested with lice] *and they threw it outside. I did not believe them however. Sanitary Committee furnished us with chicken soup—the only thing I relished.*

For some reason he is now being transported to the river steamer, *Exchange*.

Monday, July 25, 1864
On Board Steamer Exchange. As nurse brought me to the boat Sanitary Committee gave us a drink of sweet cider. Laid on some hay on Hurricane deck. Boat very slow and leaky. Rations very scarce.

Tuesday, July 26, 1864
On Board Western Metropolis. Got on board this boat about 9½ A.M. Comfortable beds were soon spread down with blankets for our Accommodation. Nursesis [sic] *were very kind and attentive. Waited the remainder of the day for more sick passengers, but they d* [sic] *not come.*

We can assume here that he was suffering greatly from dysentery, fatigue, malnutrition, and other various complaints that completely debilitated him to a point where he was not able to do anything but lay in a bed. His condition was evidently so bad that medical officers decided he should be sent to a hospital away from the battlefield, where he could get better care. Clerks were scarce; and when an outfit had good clerks, the officers tried to keep them. That could be one reason why his orders for transfer back to a Headquarters Company were revoked. And sending him to the hospital far away from the action indicates that they wanted him restored to health and back at work as soon as possible.

He remained on board the *Western Metropolis*. It was a wet trip. He was moved about the boat. Some officers were brought aboard, and he and the other enlisted men were moved from below decks and back up on deck in the rain, under a canopy. The officers were taken to quarters below deck. He had hardtack and coffee for supper on July 28. Night falls, and the next entry reads:

Friday, July 29, 1864
Third Pavillion David's Island, N.Y. Had supper, but a long walk for it. Good bread [soft]*, coffee, fresh beef, mustard and pepper sauce. Had no apetite* [sic]*. Landed at David's Island about one o'clock and about two o'clock was comfortably fixed in the Hospital and sound asleep. Very much fatigued tramping about.*

Davids Island Hospital (Library of Congress)

Saturday, July 30, 1864
Third Pavilion David's Island N.Y. Arose in the morning, put on my clothes and wore them until after I had eaten my breakfast which consisted of bread, butter, fresh beef and coffee. Ate but little. For dinner [lunch] *ate a little rice pudding. Splendid supper. Mush and milk, boiled egg, Cup of tea and bread and butter. Ate hearty. Laid in bed all day. Put on Hospital clothes.*

It seems his condition is not improving. His system cannot take the good food. Visitors are constantly walking about offering them homemade remedies for their ailments. The days drag on. He remains bedridden and eats very little. He is now alternately cold, then hot, then drenched in sweat.

One elderly lady visits him every so often and offers him blackberry cordial and canned peaches. His condition is similar to a severe case of stomach virus, only much, much worse and continuing day after day with no let up. The diet is potatoes, mush, beef, boiled eggs, bread, coffee, and milk. There are diseases about. The doctors and nurses know little of how to cope with them. Visitors shun the ward. It is extremely hot and humid. There are no fans nor air conditioning, just open windows that let in a breeze now and then, along with flies and other insects.

Thursday August 4, 1864
Third Pavilion, David's Island, N.Y. Read several chapters in the testament and found great comfort in communion with God upon my bed. Had cold sweat in the morning just before daylight. The lady who gave me the blackberries visited me again in the evening but she had nothing with her.

Thursday, August 11, 1864
Third Pavilion, David's Island, N.Y. Harbor. Sat up twice during the day, but a short time each. Suffering considerably with the heat. Bought a half pound of cheese which suited my taste well. A friendly soldier gave me a bunch of raisins. No lady visitors during the day.

Friday, August 12, 1864
Third Pavilion David's Island N.Y. Harbor. Put on my pants and sat up about an hour. Dr. told me not to eat too much fruit. Apetite [sic] *getting better.*

Saturday, August 13, 1864
Third Pavilion David's Island N.Y. Harbor. Put on my clothes after dinner and sat up and walked the floor about two hours, then changed my underclothing and went to bed again. Appetite getting stronger. Slept well.

Sunday, August 14, 1864
Third Pavilion, David's Island, N.Y. Put on my pants in the morning and kept them on all day. Sat up all forenoon. Lounged on my bed in the afternoon. . . . Walked out in the evening and breathed fresh air—the first time out of doors since coming to De-Camp General Hospital. Surprised at my speedy recovery.

Monday, August 15, 1864
Third Pavilion David's Island N.Y. Harbor Just when I had eaten my dinner, how much I was surprised to see father & mother come into the ward. They left home on Thursday. Father looked bad. Had been very unwell.

Tuesday, August 16, 1864
Third Pavilion David's Island N.Y. Spent the morning lying on my bed waiting for father and mother to come across the river. Told them I expected a furlough tomorrow. They agreed to wait. . . . Father and mother went over again to New Rochelle to stay over night [sic] *as no citizens were allowed to remain on the Island.*

Wednesday, August 17, 1864
Third Pavilion David's Island N.Y. Arose about five o'clock expecting a furlough to go home with father and mother, but was disappointed and they went home without. . . . Felt lonesome after father & mother left. Rained considerable during the day and the roof of our pavilion leaked considerably.

Saturday, August 20, 1864
Third Pavilion David's Island N.Y. A citizen nurse was drummed out of camp in the evening with one side of his head shaved and "Thief" on his back, for stealing money from a sick soldier.

Thursday, August 25, 1864
On the Cars [train] *Between Jersey City and Pittsburgh. Did not sleep any after 2 o'clock* [in the hospital]. *Received my furlough about eight changed my clothes & started for home on the nine o'clock train at New Rochelle. Got into New York about ten o'clock and spent most of the day at the New England Rooms, Soldiers Home, No. 194 Broadway N.Y. Was treated well. Left Jersey City about half past six o'clock. Were at Philadelphia and changed cars about eleven.*

Friday, August 26, 1864
Soldiers Home No. Pittsburg [sic], Penna. Spent the after part of the night rather uncomfortably in the cars. Were at Harrisburg about daylight. A break-down of freight cars kept us about two hours behind time. A trouble some [sic] man, who annoyed the ladies by smoking in the car, was put off by the conductor.

Saturday, August 27, 1864
At Home. Found the folks all well and very much surprised to see me so well. Slept but little during the night for talking.

He's home for a time, and war is far away. He settles into a round of visiting friends and family. He helps his father with the farm work, cutting timber and helping with repairs around the home. His recuperative powers amaze everyone. Not too long ago he was in the hospital hardly able to move.

Friday, September 9, 1864
At Home on Furlough. Meeting of the citizens to raise money to prevent a draft in our township.

While home there are discussions on the war, the state of the country, how the war will end, and other topics. He avoids these discussions because he is still in military service and does not think it proper to discuss his views with "civilians." He is seldom at home. He's visiting constantly—taking breakfast, lunch, and dinner at someone's home, seldom his own. Everything is fine. He never mentions his health.

Thursday, September 22, 1864
At Home on Furlough. Went to David's in the morning and bade them farewell. Spent an hour uncle George Criss'. . . . Went to John's and took dinner. . . . Learned in Eldersville that cousin John's folks of Burgettstown were at father's. Hastened home. Spent the afternoon very pleasantly. Bade the Cassidy family farewell and packed up my trinkets.

Friday, September 23, 1864
On the Cars [train] *Harrisburg Penn.* [The train ride is boring. He is naturally unhappy at having to leave family and friends, and the pleasant social life of a single, young, educated man.] . . . *Got on the train about 12-20. Felt very sleepy and slept most of the afternoon and night. Reached Pittsburg* [sic] *about four o'clock and changed cars immediately for Philadelphia. Number of soldiers on the train, some going home from hospitals and some to their regiments.*

Since he left on a sick furlough, he had to report to a hospital upon return from furlough.

Saturday, September 24, 1864
Satterlee Gen'l Hosp. West Philad'a. [sic] *Pa. Reached Philadelphia about seven o'clock A.M. and reported to the Medical Director on Walnut St. and was sent to the Citizen's Volunteer Hospital on Broad and Prime Streets. . . . Quite a number of soldiers sent to their Head Quarters. About four o'clock a number of us were sent in ambulances to Satterlee General Hospital in West Philadelphia. Supper being over* [by the time he got there] *an extra plate was set for me. Hospital not kept in as good order as DeCamp Gen'l Hospl. on David's Island, N.Y. . . . Men in the hospital rejoicing over an order by which soldiers were allowed to go home to vote, if able to travel and not fit for duty. Some thought that I might return again. Rather doubtful. Spent the evening quite pleasantly.*

He does not seem to associate with, or make friends with, any of the soldiers in the ward. He reads and reads, washes his socks, writes letters home. He seems very restless and uneasy.

Wednesday, September 28, 1864
Satterlee U.S.A. Gen'l Hospital West Philadelphia. Spent the forenoon reading in the New Testament and scouring my case knife. Afternoon was dull and cloudy. Read and wrote a letter to Irene Lindsey. Boys in the hospital looking anxiously for the paymaster, to get their money before going home on furlough to the elections. Did not sleep much in the former part of the night. Very restless & uneasy.

Thursday, September 29, 1864
Satterlee U.S. Gen'l Hospital West Philadelphia Pa. Surgeons took a ball [a bullet] *from under a man's shoulder blade in our ward in the morning. . . . cleaned my buttons. Considerable complaining about our rations which were very scarce.*

And so it goes day after day. By October 2, 1864, he is on clean-up detail mopping floors, arranging beds, getting ready for inspections by the Medical Director who never comes to inspect. Political discussions abound in the wards. The election is coming up soon—some discussion about the war and how well President Lincoln is doing. Evidently the medical people do not think he is ready for duty yet, or they can't find an assignment as a clerk in any outfit.

Sunday, October 9, 1864
Satterlee U.S.A. Gen'l Hosp. West Philadelphia Pa. After dinner, C.M. McCoy and I went out into the country a short distance. Concluded from the appearance of things that they are poor farmers about Philadelphia. Were in an old Orchard getting some apples, when the owner came along with his dogs and ordered us out.

Monday, October 10, 1864
Satterlee U.S.A. Gen'l Hospital, West Philadelphia Pa. Were disappointed to learn that we could not go home to vote. . . . Had the toothache all day. Applied tobacco to it and smoked one pipefull [sic].

Tuesday, October 11, 1864
Satterlee U.S.A. Gen'l Hospital West Philadelphia Pa. Were called out in the morning to elect three judges of election to open a poll here in order that we might vote. Boys treated the commissioner very badly by shouting "furlough,' furlough," while he was speaking. The motto with some was, "No furlough, no vote." Considered it my duty to vote and did vote for Congress, President, Judge and Assembly.

Friday, October 14, 1864
Satterlee U.S.A. Gen'l Hospital West Philadelphia Pa. Was transferred to guard in the afternoon. Were drilled some after dress parade. Slept in the guard barracks. Someone undertook to steal my overcoat from my pillow, but it happened that one sleeve was under my head and the pulling it out wakened me.

Monday, October 17, 1864
Satterlee U.S.A. Gen'l Hosp. West Philadelphia, Pa. Was on guard during the day from twelve to two and from six to eight o'clock. . . . The regular Lieutenant and some other man crossed my beat in a carriage. I did not challenge them, not knowing the orders, and the Lieutenant cursed me considerably.

Wednesday, October 19, 1864
Satterlee U.S.A. Gen'l Hospital West Philadelphia Pa. While on post about midnight, an officer ran my beat in a buggy and refused to halt when challenged. Guard duty too heavy to be tolerated and the accommodation for the guard very inferior. No fire in guard tent. Felt the effects of rheumatism and fever in my legs and shoulders.

Friday, October 21, 1864
Satterlee U.S.A. Gen'l Hospital West Philadelphia Pa. Two years of my term of service put in. Had no trouble while on post. Slept pretty well during the night as we were not called out to the gate until time to go on post.

Saturday, October 29, 1864
Satterlee U.S.A. Gen'l Hospital. W. Phila, Pa. New Yorkers were called out to see how many would vote here and they hooted and hollowed [sic] so that the Hose Co. were called out and threw water to disperse them.

Saturday, November 5, 1864
On the Cars [train] Between Philadelphia and Pittsburgh. Went on post at twelve and stood until two o'clock. On post again at six but received my furlough before eight. Went to the depot and got our transportation. Left Philadelphia on a special train about three o'clock. Train moved slowly. Some very vulgar conversation in the cars. . . . Slept some during the night. Great many soldiers going home on furlough. Weather cold. Snowed some in the afternoon.

Evidently this was the furlough to go home and vote that he had written about in earlier entries. He was met at the train at Mingo Junction, Ohio, by his father and mother in a wagon and was driven home.

Tuesday, November 8, 1864
At Home on Furlough. Attended the election in Eldersville and after I had voted I went to John's [a cousin] *and found that they were not at home. Unfastened the door, went in and ate some dinner. . . . Election passed off quietly. Some illegal votes cast and some talk of contesting the election.*

Now he's at home on furlough to vote. He has voted and begins his rounds of visiting and socializing, plus helping with chores around the farm. He visits a couple of the schools and observes the teaching going on. He is interested in becoming a teacher when he finally gets out of the army.

Thursday, November 24, 1864
On the Cars [train] *Near Harrisburg Pa. Arose about two o'clock, took breakfast, bade the folks farewell and Will took me to Steubenville, with one horse between us. Left S~ at 6½ o'clock; arrived at Pittsburg* [sic] *at 11½, procured transportation and left on the 12½ train for Philadelphia. Very fine & comfortable car. Some stealing done by the boys on the cars at Harrisburg 12½ at night. Slept nearly all night. Weather very cold.*

He arrived at Satterlee General Hospital in West Philadelphia about 5 A.M. on November 25, 1864. He was assigned right back on guard duty, then this entry:

Friday, December 9, 1864
Satterlee U.S.A. Gen'l Hospital, W. Philadelphia, Pa. Drilled from 1½ to 2 o'clock P.M. Stood guard over some men who were to be sent to the front and went with some of them to the baggage room for their baggage.

Going back to the front lines was not the most popular thing to be doing. Some men would try to escape this transfer to the front. That's why guards were put over them.

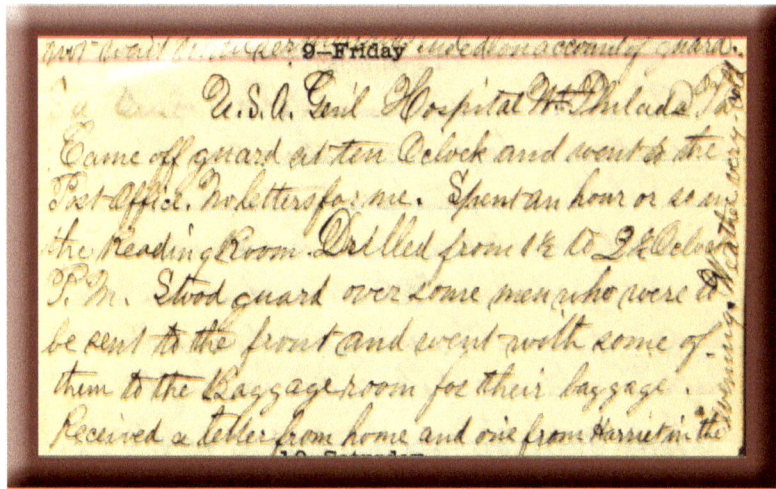
December 9, 1864: Guarding men heading to the front lines

Saturday, December 10, 1864
Satterlee U.S. Gen'l Hospital, W. Philadelphia, Pa. Went out to guard mounting in the morning and the guards were divided into reliefs. Soon after, we were called into line and marched and countermarched into Ward "W" where we were examined, and the greater portion of us marked for the front and kept under guard. A number of the boys got out and went downtown. . . . Slept in Ward "W" in lousy [infested with lice] *beds. Some of the boys took a lousy sheet before the examining board. Weather cold. Snow on the ground.*

Sunday, December 11, 1864
Satterlee U.S.A. Gen'l Hospital W. Philadelphia Pa. Spent the day in Ward W under guard waiting to be sent to the front. . . . Read some in my bible. . . . Could not get out to go even to the Post Office or to church in the chapel. Some of the boys did some washing during the day and some spent their time scuffling and playing cards. Rained nearly all day. Night very cold.

Monday, December 12, 1864
On the Cars [train] *Between Philadelphia & Balto. Received my discharge from Satterlee Hospital about ten o'clock. Some of the boys started with hospital blankets but had to leave them. Took dinner at the Provost Marshal's on 5th and Buttonwood streets. Some boots and shoes stolen as we passed through the city. . . . Some of the boys stole a hog which was hanging at a station. Weather extremely cold and snow on the ground.*

Tuesday, December 13, 1864
Washington D.C. Arrived in Baltimore about 3 o'clock A.M., took breakfast at the Union Relief Rooms about 7. . . . Left B about noon in boxcars. Arrived in Washington about 4 o'clock P.M. Spent the night in Soldiers Rest. Good supper of bread, meat and coffee. Slept on the floor.

Wednesday, December 14, 1864
Camp Distribution, Alexandria, Va. Left Washington D.C. about half past nine o'clock A.M. in box cars. Reached Camp Distribution about half past eleven. Orders very strict in the barracks. No beds on the bunks. "Hard Tack" and rice soup for dinner. Drew a knapsack in the afternoon and changed my clothing. Got a piece put on the heel of my boot. Roll-call at 8½ P.M. Met Sam M. Fowler of Co. A, 100th P.V.V. in the barracks.

Thursday, December 15, 1864
On Board the "Corsack" Between Alexandria & Fort Monroe. Left Camp Distribution about 12½ o'clock after drawing about two days rations. Put on board the steamer "Corsack" about 4½ o'clock. Were stowed away on the lower deck. Sam Fowler and I spent the night together. Slept on the floor. Wind very cold and the deck of the boat somewhat open. Slept pretty well considering the position.

Friday, December 16, 1864
"Bull Pen" City Point Va. Arose about eight o'clock on board the Corsack. Water running about our bed. Met Lieut. Stocking on board the steamer. His left arm was off. Landed at City Point about half past two o'clock and were put in the yard and barracks called the "Bull Pen." Plenty to eat. In hearing of artillery.

Saturday, December 17, 1864
"Bullpen" City Point Va. Spent the day in my barracks reading my bible and writing some in my diary. . . . Barracks crowded full of men on their way to the front. Drew pork, coffee and "Hard Tack" for breakfast and bean soup about three o'clock for dinner. Bought fifty cents worth of bread and butter. . . . Felt as though we were getting toward the front when I noticed my dirty hands and face.

Sunday, December 18, 1864
Co. A 100th P.V.V. Near Petersburg, Va. Went to Corps Head Qarters [sic] and from there to Division, Brigade and Regimental H Qrs. Reached the Company as it was getting dark.

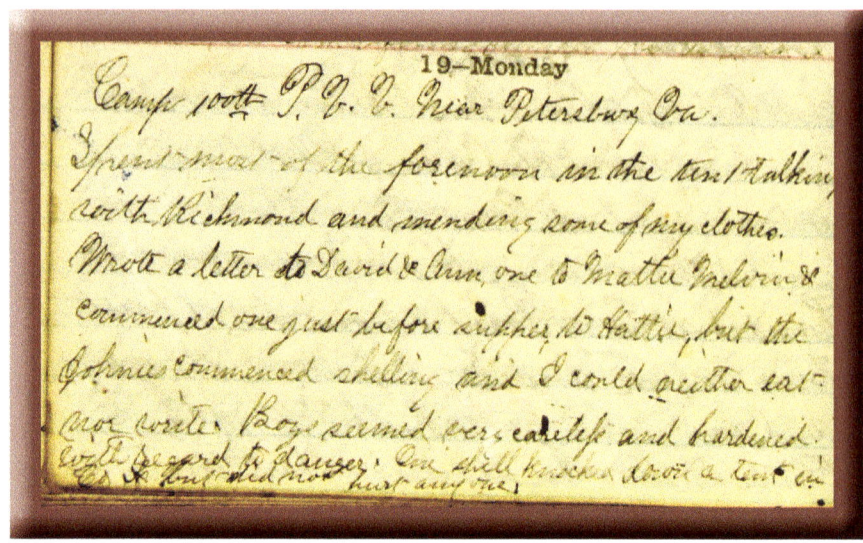

December 19, 1864: Getting fired on again

Monday, December 19, 1864
Camp 100th P.V.V. Near Petersburg, Va. Wrote a letter to David & Ann, one to Mattie Melvin & commenced just before supper to Hattie, but the Johnies [sic] commenced shelling and I could neither eat nor write. Boys seemed very careless and hardened with regard to danger. One shell knocked down a tent in Co. A. but did not hurt anyone.

Tuesday, December 20, 1864
Camp 100th P.V.V. Near Petersburg, Va. Finished writing a letter to Mattie E. Melvin in the forenoon and at fifteen minutes before three o'clock in the afternoon went on "Quarter Guard" and stood two hours to watch the movements of the Rebels. J. Barr paid us a visit in the evening and he and I had quite a chat; He informed me that he thought he could get me detailed again as a clerk at Corp Head Quarters. Four deserters [rebels] came in on our picket line at night. A great number at Head Quarters during the day.

Wednesday, December 21, 1864
Camp 100th P.V.V. Near Petersburg, Va. Two years and two months in the United States Service. Stood on guard with Sergt. Billings from three until five o'clock in the morning and stood quarter guard from seven until nine. Rained from one in the morning until afternoon.

Friday, December 23, 1864

Camp 100th P.V.V. Near Petersburg, Va. Went on picket with J. Richmond, M.M. Bell, and D. Templeton. The night was clear and cold and we were obliged to leave our pit to get wood to make a fire. Considerable of firing about the time we came on post. New troops supposed to be in the Rebels Riflepits.

Saturday, December 24, 1864

[Christmas Eve on the front lines.] *Camp 100th P.V.V. Near Petersburg Va. Spent the day on picket. About daylight we cut down a small pine tree for firewood* [not for a Christmas tree] *and got it cut up without being shot at. Read som* [sic] *in my bible during the day. Slept about two hours in the afternoon. Were relieved about 6½ o'clock. Johnies* [sic] *did not shoot at us when we were relieved. Some of the boys sang loyal, patriotic songs. No shooting during the singing.*

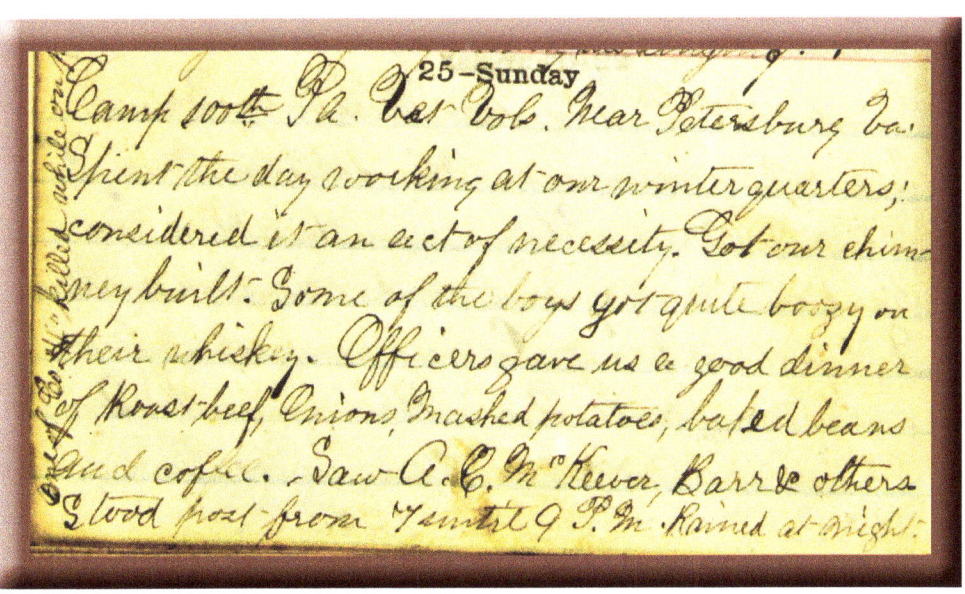

Samuel's entry for Christmas Day, 1864

Sunday, December 25, 1864

[Christmas day, a Sunday. No mention of it being Christmas. Survival was the order of the day.] *Camp 100th Pa. Vet. Vols. Near Petersburg, Va. Spent the day working on our winter quarters; considered it an act of necessity. Got our chimney built. Some of the boys got quite boozy on their whiskey. Officers gave us a good dinner of roast beef, onions, mashed potatoes, baked beans, and coffee. . . . One of Co. "H" killed while on picket.*

Monday, December 26, 1864

Picket Post Camp 100th Pa. Vet. Vols. Near Petersburg, Va. Salute of 100 guns fired in the morning over the news of the taking of Savannah by Sherman. . . . Went on picket in the evening . . . Bell acted very silly and had the ill will of all on the post. Very little picket firing during the night. Johnies [sic] *sang us two or three songs during the night and some of our boys sang in return.*

Union Army Headquarters in Petersburg, Virginia, circa 1864.
When Samuel was assigned to Headquarters Company in Petersburg, Virginia, this is where he would have worked.
(Library of Congress)

Tuesday, December 27, 1864

Camp 100th Pa. Vet. Vols. Near Petersburg, Va. Spent the day on picket. Had to keep pretty low during the day to be out of sight. Had a few words with M.M. Bell and gave him to understand that I would not be fooled with. Some shelling done in the evening.

Saturday, December 31, 1864

Camp 100th P.V.V. Near Petersburg, Va. A Discussion arose among us concerning New Years dinner for our mess, and finally I sent for a dollars [sic] worth of cookies and apples. Bought three dollars worth of eatables in our mess. Went on guard 11½ o'clock and stood until two in the morning . . . Some heavy shots fired by the Rebels about twelve o'clock.

"The Dictator" was a 13-inch mortar in Petersburg, Virginia, circa 1864. (Library of Congress)

And so 1864 ends.

He is camped near Petersburg, Va. He is on the front lines again. He is on almost continuous picket duty—out in front where the shooting is sporadic, but deadly.

Living depends on how well you can move without being seen. It's a matter of watchfulness—tense, quiet, deliberate watchfulness.

Sleep—when it comes—is very little, whenever you can catch a catnap. Comfort is nil. Yet he does not mention being homesick, ill, tired, or frightened.

1865: Heavy Fighting, and Finally Back Home

On the front page of Grandfather's 1865 diary he wrote the following:

Sam J Melvin, Co. "A" 100th Pa. Vet. Vols.

Should this little book be lost, the finder will confer a great favor upon me by returning it either to me or someone of the above named company. If by reason of sickness or wounds I may at any time become insensible or unable to state my case each day as marked in the within pages, I shall regard it as a great favor conferred upon me and my friends by anyone who may be so kind as to make the statement as above named, for me; And, should it be my lot to fall a victim of Death, either upon the Battlefield or elsewhere, I hereby request that he who may find this book, will send it, with other little articles which may be found upon my person, that would be regarded as keep-sakes by my friends, to my father, Whose address is

William Melvin
Eldersville
Washington Co. Penna.

Sam. J. Melvin

The front page of Grandfather's 1865 diary

Sam. J. Melvin
Co. "A" 100th Pa: Vet. Vols.

Should this little book be lost, the finder will confer a great favor upon me by returning it either to me or some one of the above named Company. If by reason of sickness or wounds I may at anytime become insensible or unable to state my case each day as marked on the within pages, I shall regard it as a great favor conferred upon me and my friends by any one who may be so kind as to make the statement as above named, for me; And, should it be my lot to fall a victim of Death, either upon the Battlefield or elsewhere, I hereby request that he who may find this book, will send it, with other little articles which may be found upon my person, that would be regarded as keep-sakes by my friends, to My father, whose address is
William Melvin,
Eldersville
Washington Co.
Penna.

Sam. J. Melvin.

The year 1865 begins in the same way that 1864 ended. He is on picket duty every day facing a rather quiet Confederate line of pickets. On occasion the men in the two picket lines call back and forth to each other. They exchange New Year salutes, and then the front becomes unusually quiet. He is asked to do some writing preparing Company rosters and other similar requests but is not officially detailed as a company clerk. He sends his 1864 diary home with a friend who is going home on furlough. He is now ready to face the new year, whatever comes.

Tuesday, January 3, 1865
Camp 100th P.V.V. Near Petersburg Va. Spent the day very pleasantly on picket.... Very little firing done except at marks among the pickets. The "Johnies" [sic] were very quiet and no effort of ours could induce them to converse with us. Felt very cheerful and happy when I came into camp and found a cheerful fire in my tent, and my messmate, Joseph Templeton with my supper almost ready.

Thursday, January, 5, 1865
Camp 100th P.V.V. Near Petersburg Va. Spent most of the forenoon in Sergt [sic] Atkinson's tent. He was endeavoring to learn my system of penmanship.... The Orderly Sergeant of Company F was wounded in the thigh while standing near the Lieut Colonel's quarters.

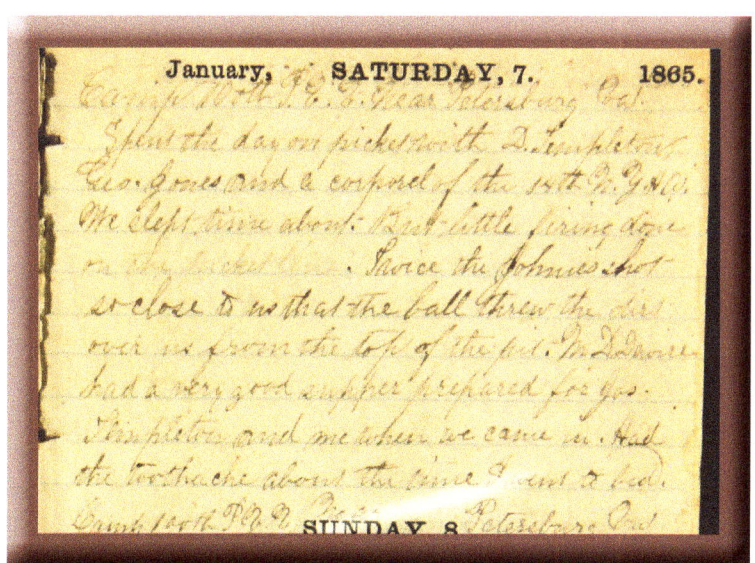

January 7, 1865: The *Johnnies* are firing very close

Saturday, January 7, 1865
Camp 100th P.V.V. Near Petersburg Va. Spent the day on picket with D. Templeton, Geo. Jones and a corporel [sic] of the 14th N.Y.H.A. We slept time about. But little firing done on the picket line. Twice the Johnies [sic] shot so close to us that the ball threw the dirt over us from the top of the pit. M.D. Dewire had a very good supper prepared for me when we came in. Had the toothache about the time I went to bed.

Monday, January 9, 1865
Camp 100th P.V.V. Near Petersburg Va. Sam M. Fowler and I went together and worked on Fort McGilvery on the right of our line until nearly two o'clock and about the time we got through One of our batteries opened fire on the Rebels and before we got away, shells were coming over the fort quite plentifully, but none of us were hurt. . . . Commenced raining between ten and eleven, and rained during the night.

Tuesday, January 10, 1865
Camp 100th P.V.V. Near Petersburg Va. Fixed up one side of our tent to prevent the mud and water from coming in. Went to the spring in the evening and stepped in a mud hole, and went in nearly to my knee.

Wednesday, January 11, 1865
Camp 100th P.V.V. Near Petersburg, Va. Went on picket with S. Fowler, L. A. Durant and John C. Ralston. Were ordered not to fire any. Rebs did not shoot and we went out in front of our pit in clear moonlight and cut our wood.

Friday, January 13, 1865
Camp 100th P.V.V. Near Petersburg, Va. A young man named Post of Co. C 140th P.V. Visited us in the evening on his way from City Point to his regiment. He spent the night with us. Had a can of oysters with him and we had them cooked after supper and had a feast. Some of the boys put some [gun] powder in Jos. Magills [sic] fireplace and as he blew his fire, it exploded and burned his face considerably. Weather very fine.

So it goes day after day—picket duty to keep an eye on the "Johnies," as he calls them. It's an effort to keep warm, but he is evidently successful at it. He is a seasoned veteran of the front now. He knows how to take care of himself and his equipment. The camp is evidently rather stable. There are no orders for quick moves from place to place. They've settled in for the winter, it seems, and they are making the place as comfortable as they can under field conditions.

Tuesday, Jan 17, 1865
Camp 100th P.V.V. Near Petersburg Va. Spent the day mostly in my tent. . . . Drew a haversack, rubber blanket, and a pair of drawers in the afternoon. Official dispatch came from Gen'l Grant stating that Fort Fisher, near Wilmington, N.C. had been assaulted and taken by Terry's Division of the 10th Corps. Particulars not received. Received orders for all men to remain in camp as the Johnies [sic] were unusually active in their pits and a move was anticipated.

A haversack is single strapped bag worn over one shoulder, used for carrying rations.

Wednesday, January 18, 1865
Camp 100th P.V.V. Near Petersburg Va. Stood guard from midnight until 2 A.M., and then wakened Sam Fowler. We had orders to keep a vigilant watch over the movements of the "Johnies" [sic] especially toward daylight.

Thursday, January 19, 1865
Camp 100th P.V.V. Near Petersburg Va. Sam Fowler went out between the picket lines and traded his dress coat to a "Johnnie" for his jacket. Traded a number of articles and got two Reb newspapers. Captain and Lieutenant of the line were both out with him.

Friday, January 20, 1865
Camp 100th P.V.V. Near Petersburg Va. Spent the day on picket post with the Lieut. and had a good time generally. Lieut. Shubert 14th N.Y.H. Arty. [heavy artillery]*, a very nice friendly man, who had arisen to his position from a private, came from Germany about the time the war broke out and could not speak a word of English; but now talks plainly. Had plenty of wood and a good fire. Johnies* [sic] *very friendly and there was no firing in our line.*

Saturday, January 21, 1865
Camp 100th P.V.V. Near Petersburg Va. Received an account of the taking of Fort Fisher. Read a chapter or two in my bible. My health very good. Nine months to serve in the army from present date.

Monday, January 23, 1865
Picket-post in front of Petersburg Va. One of the 14th N.Y.H. Arty. was drummed out of camp in the afternoon for desertion branded on the left hip with the letter "D" three inches long. Some doubts in the mind of the court which accused him about his sanity. . . . A "Johnie" [sic] *came over to the next post to ours and traded tobacco and other articles for various trinkets to our boys. Heavy firing, both artillery and musketry on the right of our line; but we did not know what for. Continued during the night.*

Tuesday, January 24, 1865
Camp 100th Pa. Vet Vols Near Petersburg Va. Spent the day pleasantly on picket. "Johnnie" called over to us in the morning, "Yank! Ho Yanks! Are you going to shoot today?" We answered "No" and kept the bargain. Heard when I came to camp that the Reb's gunboats came down the river and were shelled by our land batteries. One sunk, one disabled and three grounded. Gen'l Meade reported relieved from the Command of the Army of the Potomac.

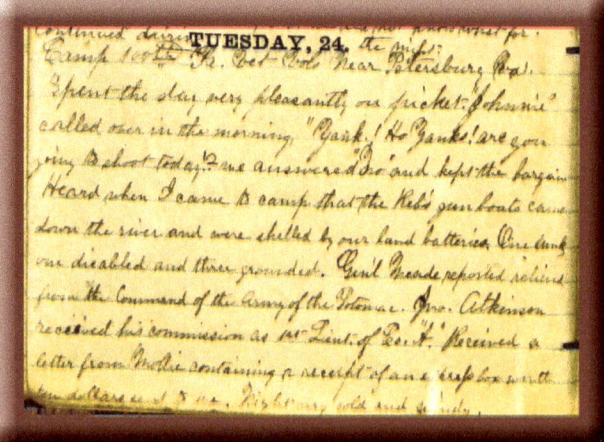

January 24, 1865: Bargaining with the *Johnnies*

Saturday, January 28, 1865
Camp 100th P.V.V. Near Petersburg Va. Spent the day on post and suffered considerably with the cold. When I came to quarters, I found an express box which had been sent to me from home. A can of molasses in it had become unsealed and the molasses was all over the contents of the box. Heard that General Burnside had command of the Middle department and that we were likely to be relieved and sent thither. The weather was very cold, but thoughts of home and a pleasant fire made the eveng [sic] pass pleasantly.

Sunday, January 29, 1865
Camp 100th P.V.V. Near Petersburg Va. Visited Alex. Adams in the hospital. When we returned and were eating supper we heard great cheering both among the Rebs and our own men and on going out, beheld both breastworks covered with men. A flag of truce was then passing, but among the various reports, we could not learn the real object for which it came.

Wednesday, February 1, 1865
Camp 100th P.V.V. Near Petersburg Va. Were cleaning up about our quarters in the morning when we received orders to be ready to move on short notice. Spent the day and night in readiness but did not move. Some of the Johnies [sic] and some of our pickets met between the lines & had a dance; the Johnies [sic] furnished the fiddle. They were North Carolinians. Virginians were not so friendly and called the N Carolinians pumpkinheaded.

Friday, February 3, 1865
Picket-post Near Petersburg Va. My twentysixth [sic] birthday. . . . Went on picket . . . Very little firing during the night, and we had orders to capture any Johny [sic] who might come to our post to trade, as an officer had been in the habit of coming in private's dress.

Saturday, February 4, 1865
Camp 100th P.V.V. Near Petersburg Va. Spent the day very pleasantly on picket-post. . . . Some firing during the day and just before we were relieved in the evening, David Hayes of Co. B. was shot in the head and died between one and two o'clock. He left a wife and four children. He and I came to the regiment together from Harrisburg in 1862.

Sunday, February 5, 1865

Camp 100th P.V.V. Near Petersburg Va. Saw the corpse of David Hays [sic] *who was killed on the Picket line. Attended church in the 9th A.C. Chapel. . . . Some of the soldiers were called out under marching orders before the sermon commenced. When we returned to camp, received order to be ready to move at a moments* [sic] *notice and I was ordered to report to the Sutler in case of a move as I had no gun.*

Monday, February 6, 1865

Camp 100th P.V.V. Front of Petersburg, Va. Received a repetition of yesterdays [sic] *orders. . . . Received a dispatch at Hd. Qrs. 2nd Corps attacked twice by AP. Hill's command and twice repulsed. 5th Corps captured fifteen loaded wagons and fifty men including a Lieut. Col. Rebs took away part of their abattis* [sic] *in front of our division* [sic]. *An attack expected and we were ordered to sleep on our arms and cannoneers to stand at their guns with guns double shotted with grape and canister.*

What is an abatis?

An "abatis" is a line of felled trees with their branches sharpened, tangled together, facing toward the enemy. It strengthened the troop's fortifications by preventing a surprise attack, and it slowed down an enemy attack once they were within the defenders' range.

An abatis in place near Petersburg, Virginia. (Library of Congress)

Tuesday, February 7, 1865
Camp 100th P.V.V. Near Petersburg Va. Some pretty heavy firing heard upon the left of our lines, but we did not learn the result.

Thursday, February 9, 1865
Camp 100th P.V.V. Near Petersburg Va. Spent the day comfortably on picket. Slept some during the day. No firing on our part of the line. After retiring for the night we scuffled some and had considerable of fun with the mice which infested our shanty, and while we were thus engaged, Wm. H. Underwood came to our door and demanded that the noise should be stopped. He had just returned to the Company and we did not know him when he first spoke.

Friday, February 10, 1865
Camp 100th P.V.V. Near Petersburg Va. M. M. Bell left the regiment without permission and when he returned late at night, Lieutenant Atkinson had him arrested and kept him in the rifle pits until morning, under guard.

Monday, February 13, 1865
Camp 100th P.V.V. Near Petersburg Va. While M. M. Bell was on guard during the night, he left his gun, and Colonel Robertson came along, picked it up and carried it off. Weather very pleasant.

It seems to be "boring time" again. The entries indicate that the days are fairly routine. They go on picket post, watch for any enemy activity, come back to camp, eat, sleep, keep the fires going, cut wood, read, write letters, talk, scuffle, argue, fight, then this entry:

Tuesday, February 14, 1865
Camp 100th P.V.V. Near Petersburg Va. on guard in the quarters from six o'clock until coffee came. Prepared for general inspection at ten o'clock and were not inspected until two, and then the inspection was very close. A captain of the 20th Mich. was riding past our regiment was shot in the breast and killed. Considerable of shelling in the evening. Pieces of shell went through M. B. McKeever's tent. Moorhead of Co. K. mortally wounded on picket. Attended church in the 9th A.C. Chapel.

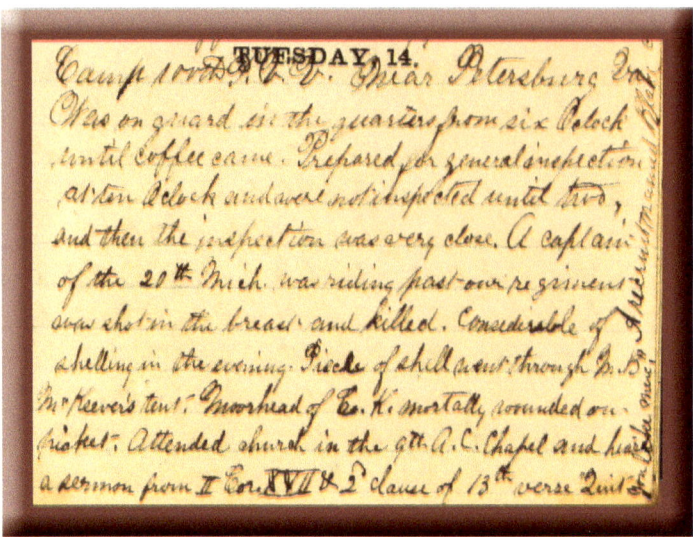
February 14, 1865: A Captain from Michigan killed

Wednesday, February 15, 1865
Picket post Near Petersburg Va. Rained all day and quit just about the time we went on picket. This having been the case several times, I almost came to the conclusion that Providence was looking with a propitious eye upon me. Spent the night very pleasantly on post with M.M. Bell and D. Templeton. No shooting.

Monday, February 20, 1865
Camp 100th P.V.V. Near Petersburg Va. Considerable of shelling done in the afternoon and the Johnies [sic] *shot into Fort Haskell several times, killing one, and wounding three. About 140 recruits came to the regiment, 12 of whom came to our company; one of them slept in our tent. . . . During the shelling one of the new recruits had a piece of his coat tail and the buckles of his knapsack shot away with a piece of shell.*

Tuesday, February 21, 1865
Camp 100th P.V.V. Near Petersburg Va. Five more recruits came to our company. One of the recruits who came to Co. B. was found to be a man who had deserted from the company just before the South Mountain fight. . . Had roll-call [sic] *at tat-too first time since I returned to the regiment.* [Tattoo is a bugle call played in the evening in the British Army and the United States Army.] *Three of the recruits absent without leave* [AWOL] *since last night.*

Friday, February 24, 1865
Camp 100th P.V.V. Near Petersburg Va. [He's trying to get some rest, but with the shelling and the frightened new recruits, it's not easy.] *Spent nearly all day making a picture frame for S. Alma Thorley. Considerable of shelling done in the afternoon and some of them lit very close to our quarters. Dispatch read to us announcing the capture of Willmington* [sic]. *A salute of 100 guns fired in honor of the event.*

Saturday, February 25, 1865
Camp 100th P.V.V. Near Petersburg Va. Spent most of the day cleaning my gun. . . . Reported by deserters that the Johnies [sic] *were about evacuating Petersburg. Saw a fire in the city in the evening. Some shelling done. One tent knocked down in Co. F. Commenced making out the Muster Rolls after supper. Signed the Pay Rolls in the afternoon.*

February 25, 1865: *Johnnies* leaving Petersburg?

Tuesday, February 28, 1865
Camp 100th P.V.V. Near Petersburg Va. Reb sharpshooters at work all day. Killed one horse and wounded one.

Friday, March 3, 1865
Camp 100th P.V.V. Near Petersburg Va. In the afternoon M. Moon one of our recruits was wounded in the finger and thigh. I went for the doctor.

Sunday, March 5, 1865
Camp 100th P.V.V. Front of Petersburg Va. Spent most of the day on picket post to the right of Fort Stedman. Kept very low during the day because our post was in bad condition.

Monday, March 6, 1865
Camp of 100th P.V.V. Near Petersburg Va. Drilled some in the afternoon. . . . Sam Wilson of Co. "E." killed.

Tuesday, March 7, 1865
Camp of 100th P.V.V. Near Petersburg Va. Drilled some in the afternoon. One (Miles) of Co. E. was severely wounded just as we came in from drill. Wm. Billings commenced acting Lieut. Attended prayer meeting in the chapel near our Brigade Head Quarters. Interesting services. Weather very fine.

Wednesday, March 8, 1865
Camp of 100th P.V.V. Near Petersburg Va. Attended prayer meeting in the chapel in the evening and bought a medal for 25 cts bearing the inscription "I promise not to buy, drink, sell or give, Intoxicating liquors while I live. From all tobacco I'll abstain, and never take God's name in vain." Promised to help to carry a library from Meade's Station to the chapel.

Thursday, March 9, 1865
Picket Post Near Petersburg, Va. Spent most of the day in the tent as the weather was wet and unfavorable. While the pickets were being counted off in squads in the evening, one of the 14th N.Y.H. Arty was severely wounded in the leg. Our post was very muddy and we had no fire. Rained nearly all night.

Monday, March 13, 1865
Camp of 100th P.V.V. Near Petersburg Va. Attended church in the Brig. Chapel and when services were about half through, there was considerable of firing on the left and we were ordered to our regiments. Did not learn what caused the firing. Ordered to sleep on our arms.

Tuesday, March 14, 1865
Camp of 100th Pa. Vet. Vols. Near Petersburg Va. Visited the burying grounds of the 1st and 3rd Div of the 9th Corps and saw three bodies re-entered. . . . Sutlers ordered to City Point and some indications of a move. Enemy reported massed in our front.

Wednesday, March 15, 1865
Camp 100th P.V.V. Near Petersburg Va. When Lieut. Atkinson came in off picket, he reported the Enemy moving toward our left. Received a letter from Mary which displayed so much sympathy for me that I shed tears over it.

Reading these entries and others that followed, he indicates that they are just standing near Petersburg, Virginia, with orders to report any moves the Rebels make and repel any attempts to break out of the city. He takes his clothes to be mended. He goes to church. He draws various pieces of equipment from the Sutlers (Quartermaster Stores). The men try to make life as normal as possible while under the combat conditions of shelling and sniper fire. The outfit is being brought up to full strength with new recruits coming in almost daily. Drills and inspections continue—drills during the week and church services on Sunday.

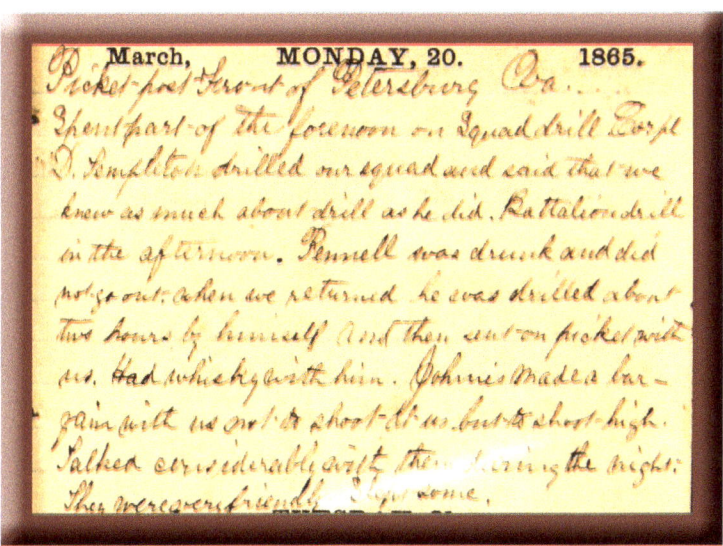

March 20, 1865: Another bargain with the *Johnnies*

Monday, March 20, 1865

Picket Post Front of Petersburg Va. Spent part of the forenoon on Squad drill. Corpl D. Templeton drilled our squad and said that we knew as much about drill as he did. Battalion drill in the afternoon. Pennell was drunk and did not go out. When we returned he was drilled about two hours by himself and then sent on picket with us. Had whiskey with him. Johnies [sic] made a bargain with us not to shoot at us, but to shoot high. Talked considerably with them during the night. They were very friendly.

Wednesday, March 22, 1865

Camp of 100th P.V.V. Near Petersburg Va. On Battalion drill in the afternoon. Lt. Billings made several mistakes and Wm Oliver Orderly Sergt. of Co. M being drunk caused a disturbance in the ranks and was put under arrest. When we came to camp, the guards tore his shirt off in trying to prevent him from escaping.

The days have dragged on. There are inspections, and casualties on the picket lines and in camp due to enemy shells and snipers. He spends his time fashioning picture frames out of wood for friends at home. It seems he has resigned himself to being a private again—a private on the front lines where death whistles through the trees in the form of rifle mini balls, cannon scattershot, or sniper fire. Then out of the blue:

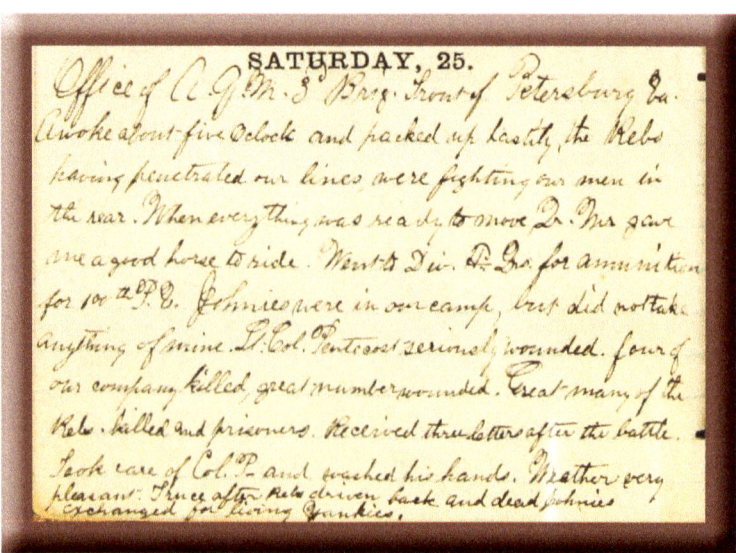

March 25, 1865: *Johnnies* in our camp!

Trail Of A Yankee

Thursday, March 23, 1865
Office of the A.Q.M., 3rd Brig 1st Div 9th A.C. Near Petersburg. Company drill in the forenoon, and turned out for company drill in the afternoon but the wind was blowing so strong that we soon came in again. Finnished [sic] writing a letter to Willie and was detailed as clerk for Capt Ladd, A.Q.M. 3rd Brig. 1st Div. 9th A.C. and reported to him for duty. Slept on rather an uncomfortable bunk during the night. Spent most of the evening in Capt. Ladd's tent reading.

    How about that! Out of the blue he is now on more pleasant duty. But he's been sleeping on the ground on pine boughs, leaves, and grass for so long that he finds a bunk uncomfortable.

Friday, March 24, 1865
Office of the A.Q.M. 3rd Brig. 1st Div. 9th A.C. Near Petersburg Va. Spent the day in the office reading, sorting, etc. Wrote until a late hour at night and did not have time to go to the regt. after my mail.

Saturday, March 25, 1865
Office of A.Q.M. 3rd Brig. Front of Petersburg Va. Awoke about five o'clock and packed up hastily, the Rebs having penetrated our lines were fighting our men in the rear. When everything was ready to move Qr. Mr gave me a good horse to ride. Went to Div. Hd. Qrs. for ammunition for 100th P.V. Johnies [sic] were in our camp, but did not take anything of mine. Lt. Col. Pentecost seriously wounded, four of our company killed, great number wounded. Great many of the Rebs killed and prisoners.... Took care of Col. P. and washed his hands.... Truce after rebels driven back and dead Johnies [sic] exchanged for living Yankies. [sic]

Lt. Col. Joseph Pentecost

Sunday, March 26, 1865

Office A.Q.M. 3rd Brig. 1st Div. 9th A.C. Near Petersburg Va. Visited the 9th A.C. Chapel in the afternoon and found it occupied by wounded Rebels under the care of the U.S.C. Commission. Visited the regiment in the evening and learned that the Rebs got through our picket line by passing themselves off for deserters with their arms, (under Grant's Circular) and thus captured the pickets. Heard that Lieut Col. Pentecost was thought to be dying.

What is a Circular?

A Civil War *circular* was a written order or directive issued by military leaders to their troops, outlining plans, strategies, or instructions during the war. These documents were used to convey important information to troops and commanders. They could also be called *General Orders*.

Monday, March 27, 1865

Office A.Q.M. 3rd Brig. 1st Div. 9th A.C. Near Petersburg Va. Heard early in the morning that Lt. Col. Pentecost was dead. . . . Sherridan's [sic] *Cavalry moving to the left of our line. Spent the afternoon and evening writing for Capt. Ladd A.Q.M. Saw an account in the Sunday morning Chronicle of the fight of the 25th. Our loss 800. Rebel killed and wounded about 3000. 2,200 prisoners taken by 9th Corps. 18th New Hampshire regiment attached to our brigade. Picket firing kept up since the fight. Dangerous relieving pickets.*

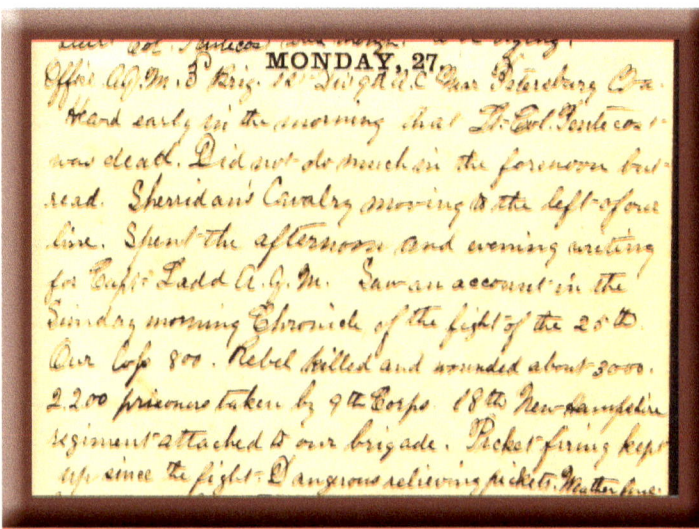

March 27, 1865: Lt. Col. Pentecost Dies

Tuesday, March 28, 1865
Office A.Q.M. 3rd Brig. 1st Div. 9th AC. Before Petersburg Va. Spent the day in Capt. Ladd's office making out Monthly Reports. Found them somewhat difficult and made a number of mistakes. Preparations seem to be being made for a move. Grant's Hd. Quarter Train passed and very large herds of cattle. . . . Weather exceedingly fine and warm.

Wednesday, March 29, 1865
Office A.Q.M. 3rd Brig. 1st Div. 9th A.C. Near Petersburg Va. Capt. Ladd having a boil on his face, did not feel much like working, so I was nearly idle in the afternoon. Wrote a little by candle-light [sic]. *Just after I had gone to bed and was asleep, a row commenced between the two lines; considerable of musketry, and the firing from mortar batteries was very rapid and beautiful* [colorful]. *Q.M. Dept. all packed up ready to move. Slept with clothes & Boots on. But two wounded in the regiment.*

Thursday, March 30, 1865
Off A.Q.M. 3rd Brig. 1st Div 9th A.C. Front Petersburg Va. Spent most of the day in the office writing. Very heavy cannonading heard on our left during the day, but the result was not learned. Spent the evening in the office. Rained very hard during the day. Sherman reported at Goldsboro, N. C. resting quietly and clothing his army.

Friday, March 31, 1865
Office A.Q.M. 3rd Brig 1st Div. 9th A.C. Near Petersburg Va. Rumors during the day that our Brig. were to charge the enemy's works tomorrow morning, but was changed at night; the enemy expected to attack, and a whiskey ration was issued to the men, thus endangering not only the army, but also the country in my estimation.

Saturday, April 1, 1865
Office Asst. Q. Master 3rd Brig. 1st Div. 9th A.C. Front of Petersburg Va. Various reports during the day concerning fighting on portions of our line. Very heavy shelling commenced about 10 P.M. and was kept up during the night. Packed every thing up and slept but little. Capt. Ladd A.Q.M. on Staff Duty.

April 2, 1865: A bad day for the Rebs

Sunday, April 2, 1865

Office A.Q.M., 3rd Brig. 1st Div., 9th A.C. Near Petersburg, Va. After nearly an entire night's shelling the morning opened up with heavy musketry and hard fighting continued during the day. Fort Mahone of the Rebel line mounting 13 guns 4 of which were 32 pounders was captured in the forenoon and held against 8 different assaults of the enemy. We had in the fort 500 sharpshooters armed with 7 and 16 shooting rifles. The Rebs were fooled by a Yankee trick. Some of our men were sent out and made a show of cutting their abattis, accordingly a force was massed there to prevent it and an attack was made on that portion of their line from which they drew their reinforcements. A great number of prisoners were captured during the affair and the Rebs suffered severely in killed and wounded. Our casualties were reported small. Brevet Maj Gen'l Robt. B. Potter was killed. Sherridan [sic]*, with his cavalry succeeded in getting in the rear of Petersburg and rendered the position untenable by the Johnies* [sic]*, and consequently in the after part of the night they evacuated, leaving their camps and garrison, equipage, guns, etc. in our possession. The 100th P.A. Vols was not much engaged during the day and had no casualties that I heard of.*

April 1865, the Fall of Petersburg (Library of Congress)

Monday, April 3, 1865

Hd. Qrs. 3rd Brig. 1st Div 9th A.C. Petersburg Va. About daylight tremendous cheering was heard and rockets seen going up into the air. We soon learned that Petersburg was in our hands, the Rebels having left precipitately, leaving their guns and camp equippage behind them. The Stars and stripes were soon flying over quite a number of buildings. Saw a great number of prisoners pass our quarters. Soon learned that Richmond was also evacuated. Packed up our tents and moved into Petersburg in the evening. Took up our abode on Dunn's Hill. Occupied a small house which had bunks in all ready for us to sleep on. As we were coming in, Packard, the Wagon master asked some wenches [girls] where they were going, when one replied, "Out into the country; the roads clear now and we's free to roam." Petersburg presented a cheerful appearance and all seemed glad to see us, both black and white; The surrounding country was beautiful. Fruit trees in bloom and grass becoming quite green. Guards were placed on the bridges so that one could not visit the city during the night. The house on the hill where Lee had his Hd. Qrs. was a most beautiful situation.

Captured Rebel Camp near Petersburg, VA (Library of Congress)

Tuesday, April 4, 1865
Office A.Q.M. 3rd Brig 1st Div 9th A.C. Near Petersburg, Va. Spent the forenoon on Dunn's Hill. Gathered up some papers belonging to the Reb Signal Corps from which I supposed our Signal Corps might learn to read their dispatches. Packed up about noon and re-crossed [sic] the Appomatox [sic], passed through Petersburg and went into quarters about a mile west of the city. Spent the night very comfortably in a deserted private farm house. Very neat and clean, but every kind of furniture taken out. Saw Roger A. Prior and saw his residence. Parties of our division were engaged in the afternoon in burying Rebels killed in Sundays [sic] fight. Capt. Ladd's Servant, William Harris, a free colored man left him in the evening and went to his friends in Petersburg where he came from during the siege. . . . Baggage wagons lightened in the evening, and eight days rations drawn preparatory to a long march. Reported by some "Lee has surrendered with 20,000 men."

Wednesday, April 5, 1865
Hd. Qrs, 3rd Brigade, 1st Div. 9th A C. on the road west of Petersburg, Va. Packed everything up in the morning and prepared to move not knowing whither. About twelve o'clock we started and moved very slowly, all the First Division teams and some of the troops being on the road. About midnight we "brought up" about nine miles from Petersburg, pitched our tents, and were about going to sleep when the order came, "Pack up." We packed up, moved a few rods, spread down our blankets and spent the rest of the night. Rode one of Capt. Ladd's horses during the day.

Thursday, April 6, 1865

Office A.Q.M. On South Side R.R. West of Petersburg Va. Packed up about 8 o'clock A.M. and started with the understanding that we were going into camp three or four miles ahead, instead of that we went about fifteen. One of Alex Aiken's lead mules went over a bridge and fell about ten feet. Was not hurt. Rode Capt. Ladd's iron grey horse nearly all day. Got into camp about four o'clock P.M. Pitched our tents. Visited the regiment in the evening. Found the boys very tired. Heavy cannonading [at] a distance in the afternoon. Weather very fine.

Friday, April 7, 1865

Hd. Qrs, 3rd Brig. 1st Div. 9th A.C. 25 Miles west of Petersburg, Va. Moved our tent and raised it a little from the ground. Capt. Ladd, the wagon master, with two teams and some guards went into the country and brought in some corn, sheaf oats and corn blades [corn stalks]. The effects of the war not seen much yet on this part of the country. Plenty of fences, stock and poultry. Rode to Division train in the evening as orderly. Visited the 100th regiment near Brigade Hd. Qrs.

Saturday, April 8, 1865

Office A.Q.M. 3rd Brig 1st Div. 9th A.C. 25 miles W. of Petersburg, Va. Did not have much to do in the office as Capt. Ladd was out foraging. . . . Cars [train] ran past our quarters during the day. One train of flats [flat cars] had large tents pitched on it for the accommodation of the R.R. [railroad] hands of whom there were about 500. Capt. Ladd accused by Lieut. Billings of having violated a Safe guard on a man's house and robbing the premises of forage, etc. Proved to be a mistake, and some one from the Div. train was the guilty party. Good news recd from the front. Generals and 14,000 prisoners captured today.

Sunday, April 9, 1865

Hd. Qrs. 3rd Brig. 1st Div. 9th A.C. Beasley House W. Petersburg, Va. Spent a portion of the day in the Quartermaster's office writing. Quartermaster out after forage. Spent the evening until a late hour writing. 1750 prisoners passed our quarters going toward City Point. 24 cars loaded with troops passed going toward the front. The 100th Regiment P.V.V. moved from the Beasley House a few miles toward the front. Felt very lonesome all day. . . . Citizens coming in for vouchers for the forage gathered to our train.

Monday, April 10, 1865

Hd. Qrs. 3rd Brig 1st Div. 9th A.C. Beasley House Va. 25 M. W. of Petersburg. Spent most of the day in the office. Made out a long report and carried it on foot to Division Quartermaster. Capt. James Galt. Capt Ladd and men are out foraging. Trains heavily laden moved very slowly along the South Side Rail Road, it being in bad condition. Heard about 4 P.M. that at 2 P.M. Gen'l. Lee surrendered himself, the Arny of Northern Virginia consisting 30,000 men with all their arms, accoutrements, Quartermaster's store, etc. to Gen'l. Grant. At first the news seemed to be too good & was scarcely credited by the men in the train although just such news had been expected for several days; But when Capt. Ladd A.Q.M. came in, he went to Brig. Hd. Qrs. & read the official dispatch, and reported it true. Prisoners parolled and permitted to go home after taking the Oath of Allegiance. Gen'l. Grant said to have gone to City Point to confer with President Lincoln. . . .Our party found plenty of forage on a certain Rebel Colonel's plantation.

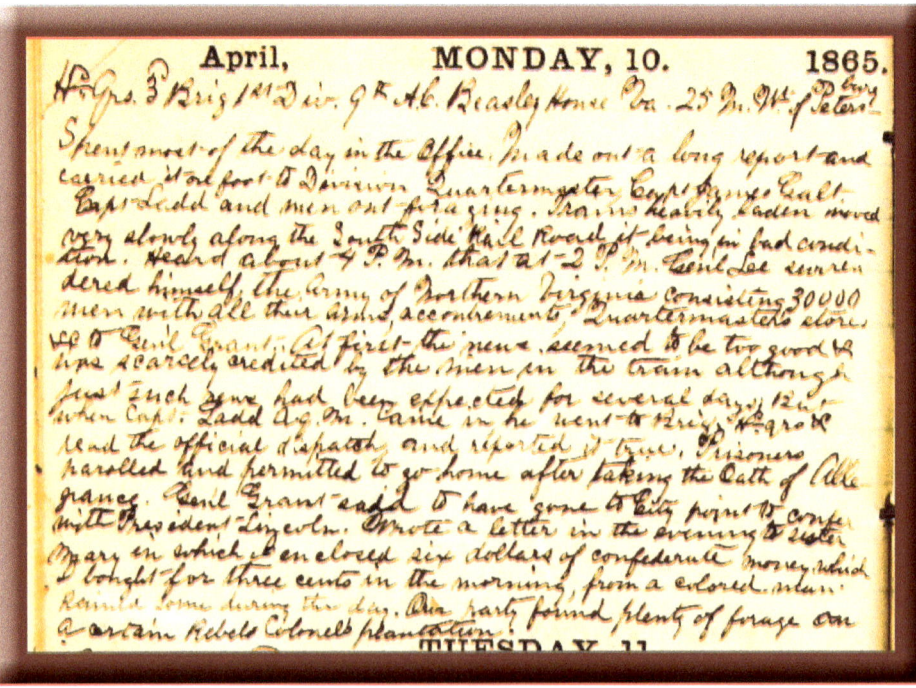

April 10, 1865: General Lee surrenders

The McLean House in Appomatox, Virginia, where General Lee surrendered. (Library of Congress)

General Lee surrenders the Confederate Army as General Grant and other Union officers look on. (Library of Congress)

Tuesday, April 11, 1865

Office A.Q.M. 3rd Brig. 1st Div. 9th A.C. Beasley House Va. Spent a portion of the day doing Office duties. 8,750 prisoners of war passed our quarters going toward Petersburg. Quite a of number of troops, among whom was some colored, passed going to the front. Two regiments of Cavalry encamped near us over night and drew forage from Capt. Ladd A.Q.M. for their horses and mules. Engineer train passed going to the front. No mail, No papers and got no news. Day cloudy and I felt somewhat lonesome.

Wednesday, April 12, 1865

Hd. Qrs, 3rd Brig. 1st Div. 9th A.C. Beasley House Va. This day four years ago the Rebels fired on Fort Sumpter. Lacked two days of being four years from that time untill [sic] Lee surrendered. . . . Talked to a School teacher of the neighborhood in the morning whose schollhouse [sic] had been shamefully abused by some of our men. Learned from him the mode of cultivating tobacco. Teams out after forage. Very windy day.

Sunday, April 16, 1865

Office A.Q.M. 3rd Brig. 1st Div 9th A.C. near Wilson's Station, Va. Heard in the evening that Pres. Lincoln, Sec. Seward and his son had been assassinated in Ford's Theatre on the night of the 14th. Pres. died at 7-30 A.M. 15th. Seward likely to recover, Son's case hopeless. Valandigham, Seymour, & the Woods under arrest as accomplices of the deed and J. Wilks [sic] Booth as the perpetrator.

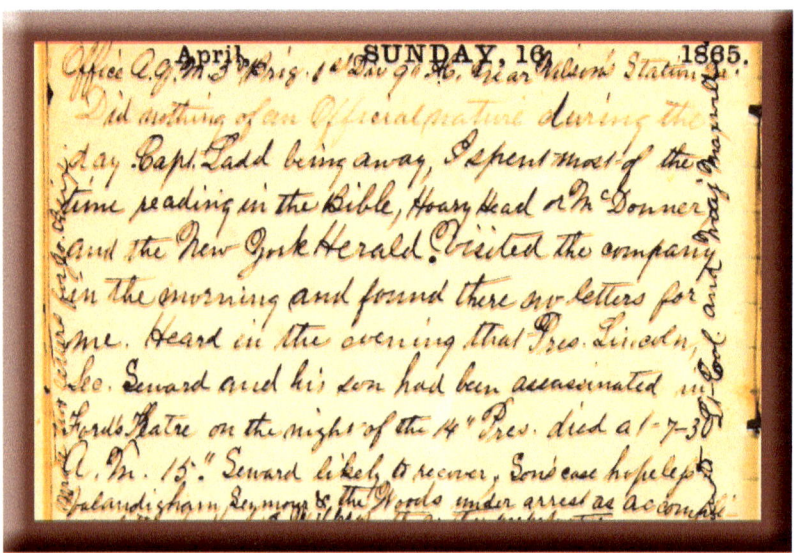

April 16, 1865: President Lincoln assassinated

108 *Trail Of A Yankee*

Monday, April 17, 1865
Office Asst. Q.M. 3rd Brig. 1st Div. 9th A.C. Near Wilson's Station Va. Heard during the day, that the paroled prisoners had attempted to blow up the Magazine [ammunition stores] *at City Point Va. Quite a number of troops passed going toward Burkesville in the morning.*

City Point Magazine Explosion (Library of Congress)

Tuesday, April 18, 1865
Office A.Q.M. 3rd Brig. 1st Div. 9th A.C. near Wilson's Station Va. Received a paper in the morning giving some account of the assassination of Messers Lincoln and Seward. About noon Capt Ladd received a telegraph Dispatch from Burkesville and started thither immediately. Lieut. B.F. Burard of the 59th Mass. Took his place as A.A.Q.M. Rode the gray horse over to the company in the evening and learned that Lieut. Atkinson wanted me back to the company as company clerk. Also that Capt. Bard was promoted to Major, Capt. Wilson to Lt Col. and Maj Maxwell to Colonel.

Wednesday, April 19, 1865
Office A.Q.M. 3rd Brig. 1st Div. 9th A.C. Near Wilson's Station Va. Read in the N.Y. Herald which was all dressed in mourning, a detailed account of the assassination of President Lincoln.

Thursday, April 20, 1865
Office A.Q.M. 3rd Brigade 1st Div. 9th A.C. Kidd House Va. Left Wilson's Station about two o'clock and moved on well until about ten P.M. when we went into camp on Mr's [sic] *Kidd's plantation in a wheat field.*

Friday, April 21, 1865
Office A.Q.M. 3rd Brigade 1st Div. 9th A.C. City Point Va. Two years and six months in the service of the U.S. Left the Kidd house about five o'clock A.M. and made a steady march to City Point about 18 miles. Reached City Point about one P.M. . . .The 100th Penna Vols not with the rest of the brigade. Troops embarked after dark for Washington D.C. . . . Considerable stir in our corall [sic] *during the night preparing to turn the train over.*

City Point Virginia, now known as Hopewell, VA (Library of Congress)

Saturday, April 22, 1865
Office A.Q.M 3rd Brig. 1st Div. 9th A.C. City Point Va. The wagon train was all turned over to Sheridan's Cavalry Corps during the day and quite a number of troops embarked.

Sunday, April 23, 1865
On Board the Sentinel on the James River. Counted out some Clothing Camp and Garrison Equipage in the morning and was returning to the office when I met Headquarters coming down. Regiment, and Brig Hd. Qrs. embarked on the Constitution and left about noon. I was left with the horses. Had a few crisp words with the orderly Joe Feix, who said I was left to take care of the horse and ordered me to put a sack of oats on him [feed him]. Left City Point about 5 P.M. Boat much crowded. 27th Mich. on Board.

Suddenly we have a quick shift of locations and activity. One day he is ashore working as a clerk in the offices of the Regiment, the next he is left in charge of a horse as the Regiment and Brigade Headquarters personnel embark on a river boat called the *Constitution.* But Samuel ends up on a riverboat named the *Sentinel.*

Monday, April 24, 1865
On Board the Sentinel on Chesapeake Bay. Spent the day very leasurely [sic] on different parts of the boat, having nothing special to do, I spent part of the time sleeping. Paid a cook belonging to the boat 25 cents for boiling us a small coffee pot full of coffee. They charged 50 cents for boiling camp kettles full, and the soldiers furnished the coffee. Some of the 27th Mich. had two small negroes butting each other on deck in the evening. The smaller one whipped. Weather very fair. Rain all night.

And with no explanation, entries resume:

Tuesday, April 25, 1865
Office A.Q.M 3rd Brig. 1st Div. 9th A.C. Near Alexandria Va. Spent most of the day on the hurricane deck of the Sentinel. Landed at Alexandria about 5 o'clock P.M. and passed through the city and encamped for the night but a short distance from where we encamped this night one year ago as we started on the campaign.

Wednesday, April 26, 1865
Office A.Q.M. 3rd Brig 1st Div 9th A.C. Tenaly Town [sic] *D.C. Packed up in the morning and moved about half a mile and had just got the captain's tent set up when we got orders to move again. Packed up and moved. Passed through Alexandria about one o'clock. Various reports with regard to our future destination. Some thought we are about to be mustered out. A report was in circulation that we were to be consolidated & re-organized to go to Mexico. Passed through Washington about 5 P.M. Quite a number of the boys got drunk. . . . All kinds of rumors float concerning our destiny.*

Tenleytown

Tenleytown is an historic neighborhood in northwest Washington, D.C. In 1790, locals began calling the neighborhood "Tennally's Town" after area tavern owner John Tennally. Over time, the spelling evolved, and by the 19th century the area was known by its current name, *Tenleytown*.

In the next few entries, you'll see that Samuel wasn't sure how to spell that name. He spelled it: Tennallytown, Tanaly Town, and Tenly Town.

The correct spelling is Tenleytown.

Thursday, April 27, 1865
Office A.Q.M. 3rd Brig 1st Div 9th A.C. Near Tenaly Town [sic] *D.C. Read of the capture of the assassin Booth & Harrold. Visited the Regiment in the evening & asked Lieut Atkinson to have me brought back to the company.*

Saturday, April 29, 1865
Office A.Q.M. 3rd Brig. 1st Div. A.C. Near Tenly Town [sic] *D.C. Morning Chronicle contained an order concerning the discharge of the army. News very good. Official account of Joe Johnson's surrender. Quarter master issued quite an amount of Clothing Camp and Garrison Equipage to the different regiments. . . . Captain Ladd and some of the boys exercised some by throwing an axe in the evening.*

The days roll by. Routine office work keeps him busy. The activity is that of an army marking time. Reports are written up and sent to various places. Inventories are prepared. Things are quiet.

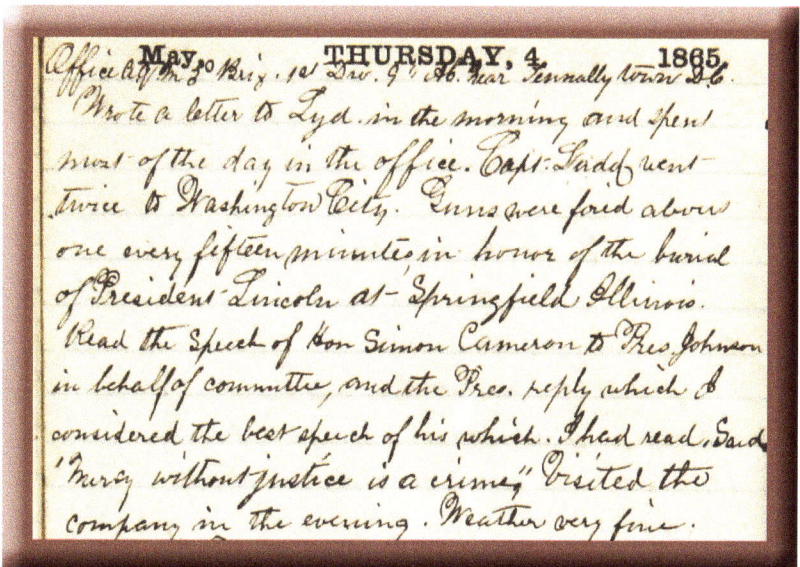

May 4, 1865: Honoring President Lincoln

Thursday, May 4, 1865
Office A.Q.M. 3rd Brig 1st Div. 9th A.C. Near Tennallytown [sic] D.C. Guns were fired about one every fifteen minutes in honor of the burial of President Lincoln at Springfield Illinois. Read the speech of the Hon Simon Cameron to Pres. Johnson in behalf of committee, and the Pres. reply, which I considered the best speech of his which I had read. Said, "Mercy without justice is a crime." Visited the company in the evening. Weather was very fine.

Friday, May 5, 1865
Office A.Q.M. 3rd Brig 1st Div. 9th A.C. Near Tennallytown [sic] D.C. Some teams were at the city, and when they returned, J. J. Book, [wagonmaster] of Co. E, 100th P.V.V. was very drunk. Captain sent him to Brigade Head quarters [sic] to be punished. Capt. Ladd expressed his determination to put a stop to so much profanity in our camp, and said he sometimes wondered that the Almighty did not destroy the whole camp.

Saturday, May 6, 1865
Office A.Q.M. 3rd Brig 1st Div. 9th A.C. Near Tennallytown [sic] D.C. the Regiment in the forenoon and saw our former Colonel Leasure. J.S. Jeffrey, M.B. McKeever and Mincher, who were taken prisoner on the 25th of March at Fort Stedman, returned to the company.

Sunday, May 7, 1865
Office A.Q.M. 3rd Brig 1st Div. 9th A.C. Near Tennallytown [sic] D.C.
Brigade Dress Parade at six o'clock. After Dress Parade, J.M. Richmond, M.D. Dewire and I went to a large stream of water about three fourths of a mile distant and took a good bath. Weather very fine.

Tuesday, May 9, 1865
Office A.Q.M. 3rd Brig 1st Div. 9th A.C. Near Tennallytown [sic] D.C.
Visited the regiment in the evening and found quite a number of the boys under the influence of liquor. The Middletown boys wanted to fight Lieut. Atkinson because it was reported that he had said that the Soldiers from Middletown were all killed, and those in the company were cowards. Quite loud talk, but no blows struck.

Friday, May 12, 1865
Office A.Q.M. 3rd Brig 1st Div. 9th A.C. Near Tennallytown [sic] D.C.
Richmond visited me in the evening and said that orders were read to them on dress parade that each man should have two suits of clothes, one specially for dress parade & inspection. No soldiers to pass outside of the camp guard without a pass from the Officer of the day. All soldiers out of their tents after taps, liable to arrest and punishment.

Saturday, May 13, 1865
Office A.Q.M. 3rd Brig 1st Div. 9th A.C. Near Tennallytown [sic] D.C.
Received a long letter from Mary in the evening in which she iformed [sic] me that there were $5,000 reward offered for Bill McGregor & Harris Perine as accused of some knowledge of the assassination.

Tuesday, May 16, 1865
Office A.Q.M. 3rd Brig 1st Div. 9th A.C. Near Tennallytown [sic] D.C.
A guard was placed on the road near our quarters to prevent men from going out of camp and to arrest all men carrying brush. In the evening, two of our teams came along loaded with poles for Brigade Head Quarters. The squad was arrested by the guard and taken to Georgetown. Guard from Head Quarters arrested their own men.

Friday, May 19, 1865

Office A.Q.M. 3rd Brig 1st Div. 9th A.C. Near Tennallytown [sic] D.C. Capt Ladd moved his tent to Division Hd. Qrs. and Lieut Little had his tent put up in its place. Put up my bunk and slept in the office. . . . Mrs. Little and her daughter visited our quarters in the afternoon intending to attend the inspection but did not go as they were alone. . . . Rained hard during the night.

Saturday, May 20, 1865

Office A.Q.M. 3rd Brig 1st Div. 9th A.C. Near Tennallytown [sic] D.C. Spent the day about the office commenced keeping a running account [log] of business transacted in the office. . . . Our cook got a pass and did not return to get our supper. . . . Order of the grand review published in the Morning Chronicle.

Monday, May 22, 1865

Office A.Q.M. 3rd Brig 1st Div. 9th A.C. Near Tennallytown [sic] D.C. Spent most of the forenoon in the office. Went over to the regiment and got John Jeffrey to cut my hair and Sam W. Fowler to shave me. Wrote several passes during the day but learned in the evening that we would have to have passes from Department Head Quarters before we could attend the review. As our cook had not yet returned, I put things in good shape, and was in readiness to cook breakfast for the Lieutenant. Troops went to the city preparatory to tomorrow's review.

Fort Gaines in Tenleytown, Washington, D.C. (Library of Congress)

Tuesday, May 23, 1865
Office A.Q.M. 3rd Brig 1st Div. 9th A.C. Near Tennallytown [sic] D.C. When I woke in the morning I found that King, our cook, had returned having been absent 2½ days without leave. . . . Grand review of Sherridan's [sic] Cavalry the Army of the Potomac & the 9th Corps. Capt. Ladd sent King to Brig Hd. Qrs. under guard.

Thursday, May 25, 1865
Office A.Q.M. 3rd Brig 1st Div. 9th A.C. Near Tennallytown [sic] D.C. . . . Mutiny reported in the 2nd & 5th Corps.

Wednesday, May 31, 1865
Office A.Q.M. 3rd Brig 1st Div. 9th A.C. (Near Tennallytown [sic] D.C.) . . . Visited the Regiment in the evening. 3rd M. Vols. [Massachusetts Volunteers] *left the Brigade, and started toward home. Col. Marshall under arrest for insulting the guard by Capt. J.S. Pyle 100th Pa. Vols. Duritz, of 3rd M. arrested, drunk and sent to Brig Hd. Qrs. under arrest.*

    Routine seems to be the order of the day. Paper work, orders to write, equipment to check and dispatch, furloughs to write and have signed—all in a day's work. Sometimes it's stimulating, sometimes it's boring. Captain Ladd had been promoted, and Grandfather is working for him again. All in all, it seems that his fighting, picket-post, front-line days are over. He is now working into the dark, late hours of the night.

Saturday, June 3, 1865
Office A.Q.M. 1st Div. 9th A.C. Near Georgetown D.C. Packed up my brass in the morning and moved over to Capt Ladd's office. Was quite unwell during the day. Head Aching. Brigade dress parade by candlelight. But I did not witness it as I was obliged to remain in the office while the Captain was out. Retired about 11 P.M. [Two hours after taps.] *Saw several men intoxicated during the evening.*

    The routine continues. He begins to think more and more about home. The war is over. Lee has surrendered. He sees other outfits being mustered out of service and going home. Why not him? He is obliged to write their orders, check in their equipment, watch them celebrate returning to civilian life. It begins to wear on him. An occasional reference to "feeling

55th New York Infantry camp near Tenleytown, D.C.
(Library of Congress)

unwell" crops up in his entries. The paper work load keeps him up late and awake early. He pitches horseshoes for exercise. Other men are getting passes and furloughs, but not him. He is essential in this wind down of the war, the dissolving of the largest Federal army to date. Why? Because he can read and write!

The entries become wistful.

Saturday, June 10, 1865
Office A.Q.M. 3rd Brig 1st Div. 9th A.C. Near Tennallytown [sic] *D.C. Spent the day about the office. Made out a requisition for Stationary for Head Quarters. Pitched a game of Horse Shoes for exercise. Visited the regiment after supper. Went to the spring at tattoo and took a good cold bath, changed my underclothing and went to bed where I spent about two sleepless hours thinking about home and my future course in life.*

Tuesday, June 13, 1865
Office A.Q.M. 3rd Brig 1st Div. 9th A.C. Near Tennallytown [sic] *D.C. Capt. Ladd received an appointment as post Quartermaster in Sacketts Harbor, N.Y. and transferred the train to Lieut. Geo. E. Priest.*

Union Army Clerks at the Provost Marshall HQ
Samuel worked in a camp much like this.
(Library of Congress)

Wednesday, June 14, 1865
Office A.Q.M. 3rd Brig 1st Div. 9th A.C. Near Tennallytown [sic] D.C. Spent the day about the Office. Helped Capt. Ladd to pack up in the morning. He spoke very kindly to me as he was leaving.

Friday, June 16, 1865
Office A.Q.M. 3rd Brig 1st Div. 9th A.C. Near Tennallytown [sic] D.C. Was very unwell all day. Gathered some raspberries. No encouraging and reliable news about going home. One year ago crossed James River. Front of Pittsburg [sic].

Tuesday, June 20, 1865
Office A.Q.M. 3rd Brig 1st Div. 9th A.C. Near Tennallytown [sic] D.C. J.M. Richmond came along in the morning and I went with him to the camp of the 46th Penna Vols in the 20th A.C. Weighed 175½ lbs. . . . 46th P.V's talked very strongly of refusing to obey an order to go to Fairfax Seminary Va.

Wednesday, June 21, 1865
Office A.Q.M. 3rd Brig 1st Div. 9th A.C. Near Tennallytown [sic] *D.C. Heard that the 20th A.C. had mutinyed* [sic] *and refused to do anymore duty until paid off. Some ten, some twelve, and some having fourteen months pay due them.*

Thursday, June 22, 1865
Office A.Q.M. 3rd Brig 1st Div. 9th A.C. Near Tennallytown [sic] *D.C. Alex Akin and I procured passes and rode out about nine miles into the country North of our camp. Took dinner at a farm house in Maryland. Paid the woman 50 cts. Got all the cherries we wanted to eat and returned to camp about half past four o'clock.*

Saturday, June 24, 1865
Office A.Q.M., 3rd Brig. 1st Div. 9th A.C. Near Tennallytown [sic] *D.C. Went up to the Regiment in the evening and took supper with my old messmates. . . . G.M. Richmond came down and spent the evening with me. Some reports favorable to the 100th Penna. Reg't going home as an organization. So reported from Brig. Genl McLaughlin Comdg* [commanding] *the Brigade.*

Right now the big annoyance is that their cook is absent without leave again!

Tuesday, June 27, 1865
Office A.Q.M., 3rd Brig. 1st Div. 9th A.C. Near Tennallytown [sic] *D.C. Bought some butter and pickles from our Sutter* [sic] *in the evening. Our cook still absent without leave. Rather unpleasant living without a cook.*

Wednesday, June 28, 1865
Office A.Q.M. 3rd Brig. 1st Div. 9th AC Near Tennallytown [sic] *D.C. No mail for me. News about going home not very favorable.*

Thursday, June 29, 1865
Office A.Q.M., 3rd Brig. 1st Div. 9th A.C. Near Tennallytown [sic] *D.C. Procured a pass in the morning and went to Washington. Visited the Capitol and went through a number of the rooms among which was the Senate Chamber. Visited Smithsonian Institute and was very much pleased with the scenes which I saw there. Animals, Fowls, Fishes, and serpents. Minerals of various kinds, shells and other curiosities.*

At last, a little time off. He has a chance to see the sights around Washington town. But one wonders what does he use for money? Some of the men have not been paid for almost a year. He's more fortunate.

Friday, June 30, 1865
Office A.Q.M. 3rd Brig. 1st Div. 9th A.C. Near Tennallytown [sic] *D.C. Spent the day making out papers. Went up to the Regiment and was mustered* [to call troops together] *for six months pay. . . . No especial news concerning our discharge.*

Sunday, July 2, 1865
Office A.Q.M. 3rd Brig. 1st Div. 9th A.C. Near Tennallytown [sic]. *After reading a short time in the morning and then went to the regiment. Heard that the A.A.G. of our division had said that all veterans would be mustered out before two weeks. . . . Heard in the evening that there was an order at Div. Hd. Qrs. to muster out 8000 veterans of the 6th and 9th Corps.*

Monday, July 3, 1865
Office A.Q.M. 3rd Brig. 1st Div. 9th A.C. Near Tennallytown [sic] *D.C. Visited the regiment in the evening. Report in circulation on pretty good authority that the 9th A.C. is about to be mustered out of service. Officers commenced straitening* [sic] *out their company clothing accounts.*

Tuesday, July 4, 1865
Office A.Q.M. 3rd Brig 1st Div. 9th A.C. Near Tennallytown [sic]. *Visited the regiment about noon and found quite a number of men drunk . . . Order issued for the 100th PA to report to Harrisburg* [Pa.] *immediately. All detailed men of the 100th in the Division ordered to report to their regimental Commander immediately.* [He was detailed as a clerk to the office of the Adjutant General of the third Brigade.] *On account of preparing to move, I did not get to sleep until one o'clock.*

Wednesday, July 5, 1865
On Board Cars [train] *Between Balto & Harrisburg. Arose fifteen minutes before four o'clock packed up and went to the regiment. Regiment left Washington at 11 o'clock A.M. Reached Balto at 2-15 P.M. Marched through the city. Stacked arms and cooks made some coffee. Left Balto at 6-15. Got along pleasantly. About one o'clock at night, the women were out peddling pies at Little York. One woman gave me a pie when I told her I had no money.*

Thursday, July 6, 1865
Co. A. 100th P.V.V. Camp Curtin Return, Harrisburg Pa. *Landed from the cars near Harrisburg about seven o'clock in the morning and marched across the bridge into the city. Regt. took breakfast at the soldiers relief. Marched out to Camp Curtin in the forenoon. Col. Maxwell took command of the post. . . . Took a good bath in the canal in the evening. . . . Conspirators* [to Lincoln's assassination] *sentenced to be hung in Washington tomorrow between the hours of 10 & 2.*

Friday, July 7, 1865
Co. A. 100th P.V.V. Camp Return Harrisburg Pa. *Jos. H. Templeton and I made out a memorial of Co. A. in the afternoon and procured a number of subscribers for it. Companies M. and C. refused to go on guard in the morning but finally went. C's officers tried to make one of their men carry a log for punishment but the remainder of the company relieved him. Heavy rain in the evening. Boys drunk at night.*

Saturday, July 8, 1865
Camp 100th P.V.V. Camp Return Harrisburg Pa. *Felt rather unpleasantly during the day. Rather lonesome. Made out a descriptive list for Edward Riley who fell from the cars* [train] *on the way to Harrisburg on the 5th of July and had both his legs taken off. Took a bath in the canal in the evening. Weather fine.*

Tuesday, July 11, 1865
Camp 100th P.V.V. Camp Return, Harrisburg Pa. *No news concerning our discharge, and no mail of any account.*

Wednesday, July 12, 1865
Camp 100th P.V.V. Camp Return Harrisburg Pa. *After taking breakfast six of us from Co. A. went out to the side of the mountain and cut twenty two dozens of wheat for an old soldier of the war of 1812, who was struck with palsy. His son being sick was not able to cut the wheat and could not get anyone to hire. Got a good dinner and as many cherries and berries as we wanted to eat. One of the recruits of Co. B. had his left leg taken off below the knee by attempting to pass under the cars.*

Thursday, July 13, 1865
Camp 100th P.V.V. Camp Return Harrisburg Pa. Went to Regimental Head Quarters in the morning and made out the morning report. . . . Spent part of the afternoon washing my clothes. Went to the city in the evening with M.D. Dewire. . . . We visited the Capitol and spent near an hour up on the dome. Very fine view of the city.

Friday, July 14, 1865
Camp 100th P.V.V. Camp Return Harrisburg Penna. After making out the Regimental Morning Report Max. McCauslin and I went out about 2½ miles and helped a man to harvest. Mowed some, scattered hay, round some wheat, Helped to haul hay and mow it away. [Put it in the haymow in the barn.] *When evening came he gave us seventy five cents between us. We were not working for wages, merely for pleasure.* [Remember, these are farm boys longing for home. Now close to going home, they are glad to be out in the peaceful fields again, working on a farm.] *Fine young lady there. She raked after the wagon a short time. Spent the day very pleasantly. Got to camp at tattoo.*

Now the living is becoming easier even though he is in the U.S. Army. He still has some clerical duties, but there seems to be a freedom to come and go after those duties are done. The farm boy takes over, and it's back to the fields.

Saturday, July 15, 1865
Camp 100th P.V.V. Camp Return Harrisburg Pa. After making out the morning report of the regiment, I took a small pail and went to the mountain and gathered some berries. Stopped at the house where we had cut wheat, [and met the "fine young lady"] *and got a drink of Buttermilk. Was on the highest peak of the mountain. . . . Bathed in the canal in the evening. Weather very fine.*

Summertime, and the living is easy.

Monday, July 17, 1865
Camp 100th P.V.V. Near Harrisburg Pa. Our blank muster out rolls and discharges were received. Went to the canal and took a bath.

Tuesday, July 18, 1865
Camp 100th P.V.V. Camp Return Harrisburg Pa. Helped to Settle up the Company Clothing Account in the morning. Rec'd the muster out Rolls and orders to make them out. From the noise heard in camp in the evening there were quite a number of men drunk. 45th Regiment, P. A. Vols came into camp.

Wednesday, July 19, 1865
Camp 100th P.V.V. Camp Return Harrisburg Pa. Company A went to the city in the morning to do Provost duty. Commenced making out our Muster Out Rolls. Found it a very tedious job. Four of us worked nearly all day and did not get three copies finnished [sic]. . . . *46th Penna. came into camp. Received a note from home containing five dollars. Answered it by candlelight.*

There are no electric lights, only lanterns and candles. There are no typewriters, no computers, no fax machines, no copy machines. Everything had to be written by hand to complete all the paperwork to get hundreds, even thousands of men discharged from the army.

Thursday, July 20, 1865
Camp 100th P.V.V. Camp Return Near Harrisburg Pa. Spent the day working on the Muster and Pay Rolls. Wrote as fast as I could from half past nine A.M. until half past six P.M. and did not get it all finnished [sic]. . . . *Great many men drunk about camp although the Mayor of the city ordered the sale of whiskey stopped in the city.*

Friday, July 21, 1865
Camp 100th P.V.V. Camp Return Harrisburg Penna. Spent the forenoon making out discharges the Officers being under arrest in the city for some depredations committed in a drinking Salloon [sic]. *Our Capt., 1st & 2nd Lieuts, 1st & 2nd Sergts were all in the scrape. They came back at noon and we finished the muster out rolls and they* [the officers who were arrested] *were taken in to head Quarters.*

Saturday, July 22, 1865
Camp 100th P.V.V. Camp Return Harrisburg Penna. Finnished [sic] *writing out the discharges of Co. A and they were taken to Head Quarters to be signed by the Colonel in the forenoon. The 6th Regt of Gen'l Hancocks Veteran Reserve Corps relieved our regiment in the evening. 4th Penna. paid off and started home. A man and a woman in our camp arrested for stealing tents. Were caught with them in their wagon. Were kept in the guard house all afternoon.*

Sunday, July 23, 1865

Camp 100th P.V.V. Camp Return Harrisburg Pa. Spent the entire day about camp. Repented before night that I did not go to church in the city. Attended the M.E. Church in the evening and heard a member of the Ohio Conference formerly a chaplain in the Army, from the 28th verse of the XLV chapter [of Genesis] *"And Israel said, It is enough!" . . . . Boys all in very fine spirits expecting to be mustered out on the morrow.*

Monday, July 24, 1865

Camp 100th P.V.V. Camp Return Harrisburg Pa. Finnished [sic] *filling out the discharges of Co. "A" in the morning and we were mustered out about noon. Spent the afternoon making out papers for the officers. Capt. Atkinson had some guns more than he was accountable for and he gave them to some of the boys. . . . Weather very fine.*

And now the day he had been longing for had arrived. Day after day he had been writing discharge papers for other men. Now it was his turn.

He was going home!

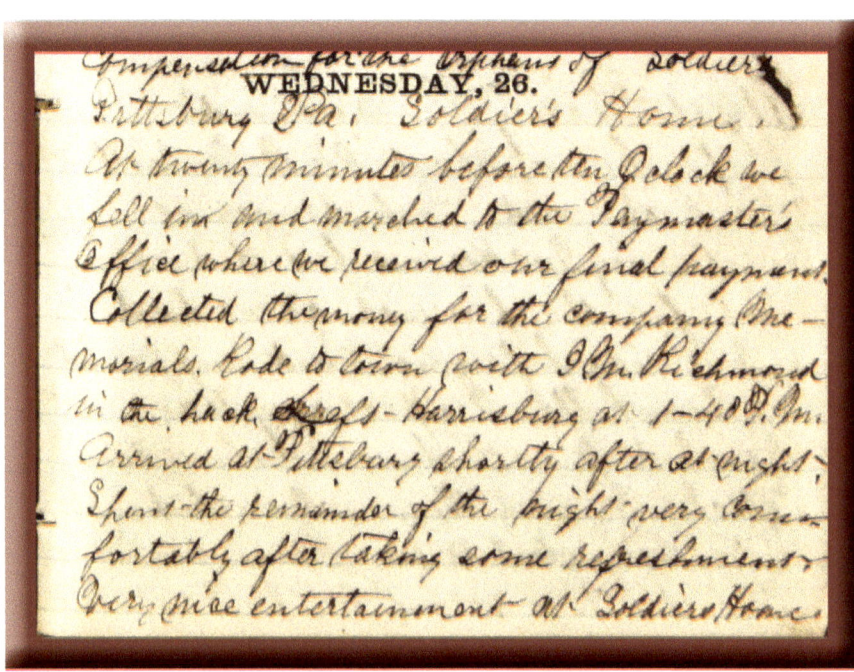

July 26, 1865: Heading home!

Wednesday, July 26, 1865

Pittsburg [sic], *Pa. Soldier's Home. At twenty minutes before ten o'clock we fell in and marched to the Paymaster's Office where we received our final payment. . . . Rode to town with J. M. Richmond in the hack. Left Harrisburg at 1-40 P.M. Arrived at Pittsburg* [sic] *shortly after at night. Spent the remainder of the night very comfortably after taking some refreshment. Very nice entertainment at Soldier's Home.*

Thursday, July 27, 1865

At Home. After taking breakfast at the Soldier's Home in Pittsburg [sic] *a number of us went to the St. Clair Hotel and left our baggage. Went to clothing stores and bought our clothing. Took dinner at St. Clair Hotel. Left P~ on the 2-40 P. M. Train. Arrived at home about 11-15 P.M. Found folks all in bed. Carried my valise from the river and felt very tired. J.M. Richmond came home with me.*

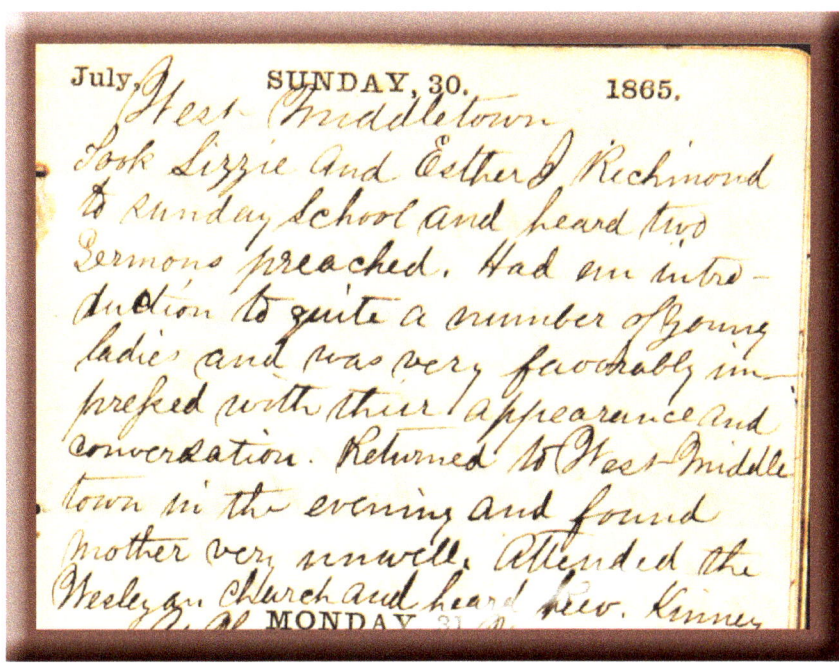

July 30, 1865: an introduction to a few young ladies

Sunday, July 30, 1865
West Middletown. Took Lizzie and Esther J. Richmond to Sunday School and heard two Sermons preached. Had an introduction to quite a number of young ladies and was very favorably impressed with thier [sic] *appearance and conversation.*

It would seem from his entries after coming home from the war that he was in the company of a number of "lovely" young ladies. After almost three years of war, civilian life and all its comforts and pleasantries are welcome experiences. He seems to settle into civilian life almost overnight.

Thus ends Samuel's military service and the year of 1865.

These soldiers are making coffee on the front lines hear Petersburg, Virginia. No wonder Samuel was happy to be discharged and back home with his family!
(Library of Congress)

1866: Back Home, and a Romance Begins

Military service in those days was tough. In fact no military experience is totally pleasant. He is glad to be home. He doesn't realize it, but he is about to enter into a new, exciting, and sometimes confusing time of his young life. It starts with this entry:

Monday, June 25, 1866
At Home. Arose at four o'clock, went to Mr. Boles' and told them of the singing at John Melvin's. Spent the day until supper-time mostly in the cornfield. Hived a swarm of bees. Attended a singing at John Melvin's in the evening. [There is no television or radio in his day. People enjoyed each other's company. They got together at church socials, picnics, family reunions, in town on Saturday nights and at other times for social events. Those who liked music and singing got together every so often for a "singing." He had gone to a "singing" at his cousin John's home. But, let him tell you about it.] *Had a very pleasant singing. Had an introduction to Miss Helen Hanlin.*

Miss Helen Hanlin was a petite, beautiful girl from one of the area's leading families. Her father owned a farm near a place called Hanlin Station, Pennsylvania. Yes, *Hanlin Station* was named for her family. Miss Hanlin, after a proper courting time, became Mrs. Samuel Jones Melvin, my paternal grandmother.

Hanlin Station, Pennsylvania

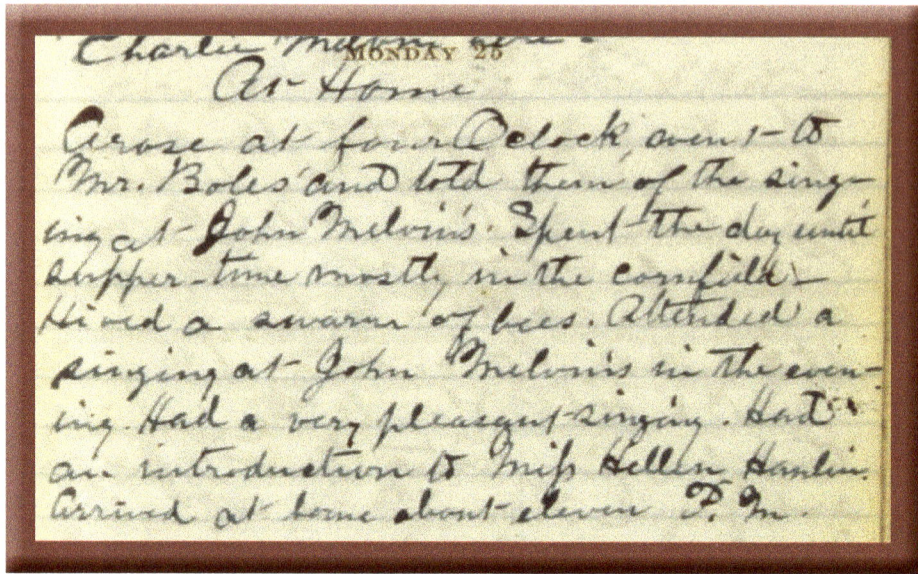

Monday, June 25, 1866: A romance begins

But that's a whole new chapter in my grandfather's life, one that would tell of his courtship of Miss Hanlin, his marriage, the birth of three boys and two girls—my father and my aunts and uncles. But, for now we leave him casting admiring glances at Miss Hanlin as they begin the courtship that will lead to a life-long, loving marriage.

He's glad to be home.

Epilogue
by Richard Melvin

Putting this book together proved to be a fascinating experience for me. I got to know my great-grandfather through the writings in his diaries. I learned that he proudly served his country, worked hard to live a Godly life, never touched alcohol, married the love of his life, and endured some terrible hardships, such as the death of his son William, when little "Willie" was only seven years old. Through it all, Samuel stayed the course, made his mark, and left us all a little better for it.

When my time comes and the Good Lord calls me home, I hope to meet my great-grandfather Samuel, shake his hand, and thank him for his service to the country, his family, and for the wonderful experience of reading his diaries.

Knowing and understanding your family's history is one of the most important aspects of life. Our family is truly blessed to have Samuel's diaries as a foundation for the Melvin family's ongoing legacy.

Copyright 2025 by Richard Melvin

All rights reserved. This book or any portion thereof may not be reproduced or used in any manner whatsoever without the express written permission of the publisher except for the use of brief quotations in a book review.

Richard Melvin, LLC
Hilliard, OH 43026

ISBN: 978-1-7349030-6-5

www.ingramcontent.com/pod-product-compliance
Lightning Source LLC
Chambersburg PA
CBHW061738070526
44585CB00024B/2721